Grac…

DEVOTIONAL … GIRLS

Inspiring Daily Devotions

to Strengthen Family, Tackle School Stress

and Build Friendships

Graceful Growth

Contents

Reader Bonus

Ready for the Next Level?

Dive into the Teen Devotional for Girls:
Perfect for Deepening Your Faith as You Grow!

Step 1: Leave A Review (Optional)

It would mean a lot to me if you could leave a quick review of

"Grace and Growth, Devotional Readings for Tween Girls!

Step 2: Claim Your Bonus

Claim your free bonus by scanning the QR code.

Just tell us where to send it!

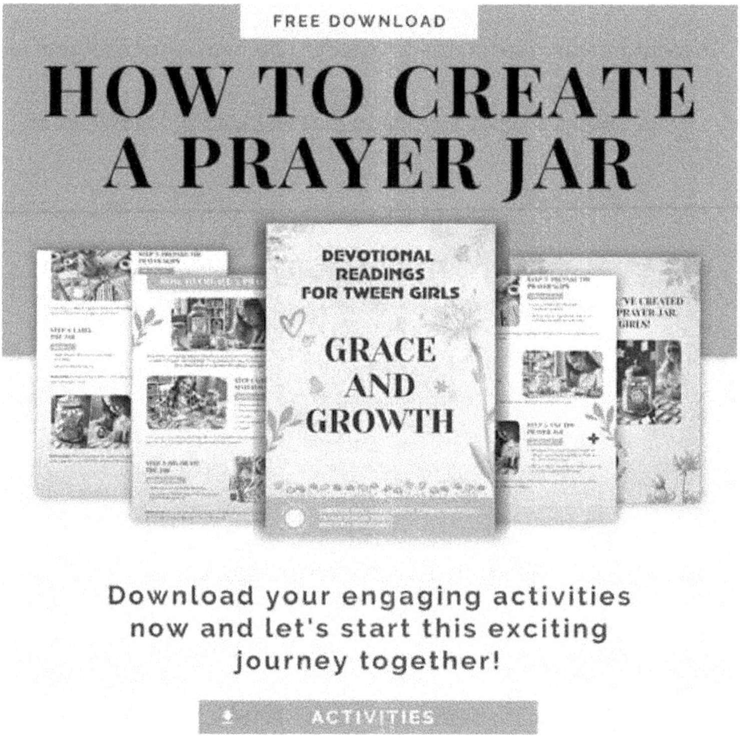

Scan the QR code.

Introduction

Have you ever felt like everyone else knows who they are and where they belong while you're still trying to figure it out? Do you feel like you're the only one still piecing things together? If you do, you're not alone. Growing up can feel like solving a puzzle, and figuring out your faith can make it even more challenging.

That's precisely why I wrote this book. I remember feeling invisible, as if no one understood what I was going through. It was tough, and I wished for someone to help guide me. Now, I want to be that person for you. As your mentor, I want to walk alongside you, not as an authority figure, but as a friend who has been through similar experiences. I'll be sharing stories and truths that can light your path as you grow in height, heart, and faith in Jesus.

Grace and Growth: Devotional Readings for Tween Girls is more than just a book—it's a shared journey. It's written primarily for you, a girl learning to trust Jesus while also discovering who you are and how to navigate the ups and downs of tween life. Through real-life stories, reflections, and practical advice, this book will help you strengthen your relationships with your family, tackle school stress with confidence, and build meaningful friendships. You'll discover how deeply God loves you, even when it feels like no one else does.

Together, we'll explore everything from understanding your identity in Christ to building strong family bonds, handling the pressures of school, and creating lasting friendships. Each chapter is designed to meet you where you are, offering insights and encouragement to help you grow in your faith and remind you that you're never alone.

As we read this book, I hope you find moments of joy, maybe even a few tears, and, most importantly, a deeper connection with God. You'll learn that no matter what challenges you face—whether at home, at school, or with friends—there's always enough grace for today and hope for tomorrow.

So, let's embark on this journey together! I'm here to listen, support, and walk with you every step of the way. Let's explore, ask questions, and grow stronger in faith, knowing we're in this together. You are not alone on this journey. You are part of something much bigger, and I'm right here with you.

Chapter 1

Discovering Self and Faith

Do you ever look up at the night sky, filled with countless stars, and think about how big the universe is? It's easy to feel small in those moments, but they remind us of how uniquely crafted each of us truly is. This chapter is about discovering and embracing the incredible uniqueness God has woven into us. Everything God created, from the patterns of stars to the details of a single snowflake, has a particular purpose and beauty—including you!

In this chapter, we're going on an exciting journey of self-discovery and faith. We'll learn what seeing and celebrating your individuality as part of God's fantastic creation means. We'll explore stories from the Bible that show the power of being yourself, do fun activities to help you learn more about who you are, and find ways to appreciate our differences without comparing ourselves to others. Let's dive in together, discovering how deeply God loves you and wonderfully He created you. Get ready for a fun journey of joy and discovery!

1.1 Created Unique: Understanding Your Uniqueness in God's Eyes

God's Diverse Creation

When you walk through a garden, have you ever noticed that no two flowers are alike? Some burst with bright colors, while others charm with softer shades, but each has its unique pattern, shape, and size. Just like these flowers, each of us is wonderfully unique. Psalm 139:14 says, "I praise you because I am fearfully and wonderfully made; your works are wonderful, I know that full well." This verse isn't just poetic; it's a beautiful truth showing that, in God's eyes, every detail of how you are made is intentional and purposeful.

Think about all the different things in nature—the many animals ideally suited to where they live and the countless types of trees, each with its role. This fantastic variety isn't random; it shows just how creative God is! Like every snowflake has its special design, you are unique and unlike anyone else. The variety in nature reflects the diversity among people—God made each of us with our special talents, interests, and unique paths in life. This incredible diversity reminds us that we are each a unique masterpiece created by God to bring something special to the world.

"Exploring nature of God's creativity"

Personal Stories of Uniqueness

The Bible tells us how God called many young people for unique purposes. Think about David, a young shepherd who became Israel's greatest king. His courage, faith, and love for God helped shape his journey. Then there's Mary, a young girl from Nazareth, chosen to be the mother of Jesus—one of the most critical roles in history. Her story shows that God sees our potential and purpose, even when others might not.

These stories aren't just old tales; they're reminders that God has a unique plan for each of us. Just like David's skills with a sling were necessary for his calling, your talents and interests are essential for your life's purpose. Whether you're great at math, making friends, or love painting, each thing you're good at is a piece of the puzzle that makes up your life and your journey with God. God gave you these gifts for a reason, so you can use them to help others and honor Him.

Encourage Self-Reflection

Consider starting a "uniqueness journal" to help you learn more about what makes you unique. In your journal, write down things like the talents you notice in yourself, the qualities people often compliment you on, or times when you feel alive and excited about what you're doing. Ask yourself questions like, "What am I good at that others find difficult?" or, "What activities make me lose track of time because I enjoy them so much?" These aren't just fun exercises but powerful ways to understand and appreciate yourself more, helping you take charge of your growth journey!

Counteract Comparison

In a world full of social media and seeing everyone's best moments, it's easy to start comparing yourself to others. But remember what II Corinthians 10:12 says: "... but when they measure themselves by one another and compare themselves with one another, they are without understanding." Instead of focusing on how you compare to others, try thinking about how you're growing as an individual. Celebrate your milestones, no matter how small they seem, and use them to mark your unique journey.

When you feel tempted to compare yourself to others, take a moment to pause and think about what you have achieved and the personal goals you're working toward. Focusing on your growth rather than comparison is essential to appreciating and embracing your uniqueness. In this chapter, remember that discovering and celebrating your unique self isn't just about feeling good; it's about seeing yourself as an essential part of God's plan, created with purpose and love to play a unique role in the world.

1.2 The Truth About Beauty: Seeing Yourself as God Sees You

In a world filled with glossy magazine covers and perfect Instagram feeds, it's easy to compare yourself to the beauty standards of media and popular culture. But what does true beauty look like through God's eyes? Unlike society's ever-changing ideals, the beauty God values is constant and shines from the inside out. Proverbs 31 talks about a woman with noble character, whose worth is far more precious than jewels, showing that natural beauty is about loving the Lord, not physical appearance. Similarly, 1 Peter 3:3-4 encourages us to focus on the inner beauty of a gentle, quiet spirit, which is precious to God.

This idea of beauty, based on character and spirit, frees you from constantly trying to look perfect. The Bible celebrates women for their faith, courage, and wisdom. For example, Esther was beautiful, but her bravery and intelligent choices in a dangerous time saved her people and made her story unforgettable. In our times, Mother Teresa's beauty wasn't in her looks but in her kindness and work helping the poorest people, showing God's love every day.

To think more about this, why not start a **"beauty journal"?** Use your journal as a private place to write down qualities that show true beauty, like kindness, courage, generosity, and faithfulness—in yourself and others. Each day, jot down moments when you felt beautiful because of something you did or said, not just how you looked. Focusing on inner beauty can help you see that what matters most isn't what's on the outside but what's in your heart.

"You're fearfully and wonderfully made"

Let's also discuss how the media influences our ideas of beauty. This is especially important for tweens, teens, and young women, who often feel pressured about their appearance. Every day, we see images and messages telling us how to look, dress, and act. These messages often suggest that you need to change to be considered beautiful.

As you're growing up, it's essential to think critically about these messages and see them for what they are. Ask yourself, "Whose standards are these?" "Do they match what God says is true and beautiful?" When you see a photo in a magazine or a post online, remember that these images are often edited and must show an accurate picture. Instead of letting these images define your worth, remind yourself of what Psalm 139:14 says: **God made you fearfully and wonderfully, no matter what the world says.**

By embracing God's idea of beauty, you can start to appreciate yourself and others more meaningfully. You'll find confidence not in following trends but in knowing that you're loved and valued just as you are. This knowledge helps you live not as a follower of trends but as someone who reflects the lasting beauty of God's love.

1.3 My Faith Journey Begins: First Steps to Knowing God

Imagine you're learning to ride a bike. At first, it might seem a little scary—you must balance, pedal, and steer simultaneously. But with time, patience, and practice, what once seemed impossible becomes a source of joy and freedom. Starting your faith journey is similar. It might initially feel unfamiliar, but as you practice, it becomes a natural and joyful part of your daily life.

Let's explore the core message of the gospel, which is the foundation of the Christian faith. It all centers on God's immense love for you—an unconditional love that never changes and is always with you. This love is so big that God sent His only Son, Jesus, to show us how to live and love. Jesus taught essential lessons, performed miracles, and then did something unique—He gave His life for us, showing that God's love is more vital than anything, even death. But the story doesn't end there—three days later, He rose again, proving that nothing can defeat God's love. This act of love gives us a chance for a new beginning and a forever friendship with God, who is always wise, kind, and with you.

Your relationship with God differs from social media friendships, where things can be shallow. It's more like your friendship with your best friend—you share secrets, spend time together, and support each other no matter what. Having a relationship with God is similar. You talk to Him through prayer, listen to Him in Bible stories, appreciate the beauty around you, and follow His guidance on living a whole and happy life.

"Meeting with other believers"

So, how do you build good faith habits? Think of them as daily steps that help you feel closer to God. Start with prayer—talk to God about your day, ask for help, say thank you, or pray for others. Going to church is another crucial step. It's a place to meet other believers, learn more about God, and be part of a community that grows with you. Just like watering a plant helps it grow, praying and attending church help your faith grow more robust.

Remember, it's normal to have questions about faith. Questions mean you're thinking deeply and want to understand more, which is a beautiful part of faith growth. To help with these questions, keep a journal to write them down. Talk about them with trusted adults, like family members, church leaders, or teachers—they can share helpful insights. There are also many books and websites for young people like you exploring their faith. These are great tools to help you find the answers you're looking for and understand more about your relationship with God.

As you take these first steps on your faith journey, remember that every step is progress, no matter how small. Like learning to ride a bike, each day brings you closer to safely and confidently riding.

1.4 Questions for God: Doubts and Curiosity

Have you ever had a question about God, faith, or life and didn't know where to find the answer? Maybe you've wondered why bad things happen to good people, what heaven is like, or how you can be sure God is listening. You're not alone—everyone has questions that don't have easy answers, no matter how old they are or how much they know about faith. What's important to remember is that having questions is a normal part of your faith journey. It shows you're thinking deeply about what you believe and growing spiritually.

Think about some of the essential people in the Bible—they had doubts and questions, too. Look at Moses, for example. Even after God spoke to him through a burning bush, he wondered if he was the right person to lead the Israelites out of Egypt. Or think about Thomas, one of Jesus' disciples, who doubted that Jesus was alive again until he could see and touch Jesus' wounds himself. These stories remind us that doubt is a natural part of faith growth. It's okay to wrestle with big questions; it's all part of getting to know God better and understanding His plans for us.

To help with your questions about faith, **why not start a "question box"**? It could be an actual box or a digital note app where you write down any questions that come to mind. Remember, writing down your questions doesn't mean you're losing faith; you're trying to understand more deeply. Take some time each week to think about these questions. Some answers might come quickly, while others might take more time and thought.

There are many ways to find answers to your questions. **Reading the Bible is a great place to start**. While the Bible might not answer every modern question directly, it gives guidance and principles to help you find answers. For example, if you're feeling scared, Philippians 4:6-7 offers advice about praying and finding peace in God that goes beyond what we can understand.

Besides reading on your own, talking to trusted adults like family members, pastors, or religious teachers can be very helpful. They've had similar questions and can share their experiences and understanding. Prayer is another powerful way to seek answers—it's more than just asking for things; it's a conversation with God where you can share your doubts and ask for guidance. Remember, prayer is as much about listening as it is about talking. Sometimes, answers come through feelings, sudden realizations, or something someone else says. Be open to recognizing those answers in different ways.

"Address your doubt by reading the bible and pray"

Talking about your questions with friends or mentors can also be helpful. Create a group where everyone feels safe to share their doubts and thoughts. You'll realize you're not alone with your questions, and these discussions can lead to insights you might not come to on your own. Whether in a youth group at church or hanging out with friends who share your faith, these conversations can be a great way to learn and connect. Exploring faith and doubt is about trusting God's wisdom and timing. Every question you think about brings you closer to a stronger, more confident faith.

1.5 Prayer as a Conversation: Talk to God Daily

Imagine having a friend who is always there, ready to listen and truly understand your feelings. That's what prayer is like when you think of it as a conversation with God. Often, we think of worship as something formal, only for church or bedtime, or feel like we need to use particular words for it to "count." But what if you thought of prayer as just talking to God about your day, hopes, fears, or even the little moments that made you smile? When you pray, it's like chatting with your best friend—you share your true self, knowing that God hears you and loves you no matter what.

Let's simplify this comforting practice with some simple prayer starters. These aren't magic words, but they can help you begin if you need help figuring out how to start. In the morning, you could say, "Good morning, God. Thank you for this new day. Help me see the good things, even if things get tough." Before a test or a challenging task, you might pray, "God, I'm feeling nervous about this. Please calm my heart and help me remember what I've studied." You could close your day at night with, "Thank you, God, for being with me today. Please give me peace tonight and a restful sleep." These starters are stepping stones to help you find your own words as you get more comfortable talking to God about anything and everything.

Starting a daily prayer journal can be fun, allowing you to talk with God more often. It could be a notebook or even an app where you write down what you pray about each day. The best part of keeping a prayer journal is seeing how your relationship with God grows! You can jot down your prayers, any answers you get, or how you feel during or after praying. Over time, as you look back, you'll see a story unfold—a tale of how God is working in your life, listening to you, and answering in ways that might surprise you!

Another essential part of understanding prayer is listening to God's guidance. This might sound tricky—how do you hear God, after all? It's not about expecting to hear a voice out loud but more about feeling a gentle nudge in your heart, a sense of peace, or even a new idea that helps you or someone else.

To improve your ability to notice these moments, try setting aside a few minutes after you pray to sit quietly. You could look out the window, doodle in your prayer journal, or close your eyes and breathe slowly. This quiet time is like saying, "Okay, God, I'm listening," and giving Him a chance to speak to your heart.

"Talking to God through prayers with heart of thanksgiving"

By praying, journaling, and listening to God every day, you build a relationship with God that can help you through challenging and happy times. Prayer strengthens your faith in quiet, powerful ways, reminding you that you are never alone. Whether you whisper, write, or think your words, God holds them in His loving hands, understanding you completely.

1.6 The Bible and Me: Make Scripture Reading Engaging

When you think about reading the Bible, what comes to mind? Maybe you picture an old, dusty book filled with complex words and complicated stories. But what if I told you the Bible could be as exciting and engaging as your favorite novel or movie? The key is to find the correct version that speaks to you and discover fun, creative ways to dive into its timeless lessons.

Let's talk about the different versions of the Bible. You might not know this, but there are several translations, each with its style and language. For example, the New International Version (NIV) is known for its clear and modern language, making it popular with readers of all ages. Then there's the New Living

Translation (NLT), which uses very casual language—great if you're starting to explore the Bible independently. If you love the beauty and poetry of words, the English Standard Version (ESV) offers a more literal translation with a majestic tone. Trying out different versions can help you find one that feels comfortable and relatable, making your reading experience much more enjoyable.

How about making Bible reading a fun, rewarding part of your day? Creating a Bible reading plan that fits your schedule and interests is a great way to start. You could start with a plan that focuses on the life of Jesus, reading a little each day about his teachings and miracles. Or maybe you'd prefer a plan that covers all the big stories of the Bible, from Genesis to Revelation, for a broad overview of the entire Bible story.

You can find these plans in books, apps, or even in the margins of some Bibles designed for tweens and teens. These plans often include readings, questions, and prompts to help you think about what you've read and how it applies to your life.

Adding some creativity to your Bible study can also make it more engaging. Have you ever tried Bible journaling? Bible journaling can mean taking notes, drawing, coloring, or even creating scrapbook-style pages in the margins of your Bible or in a separate notebook. For example, if you read a passage about the beauty of God's creation, you could draw some of the animals or landscapes mentioned in the text. This approach helps you understand what you're reading and makes your study time a creative, fun activity!

Another great idea is to connect Bible stories and teachings to your everyday life. The Bible is ancient, but its lessons are still relevant today. For example, think of David facing Goliath as more than just a story—it can be a way to think about overcoming "giants" or significant challenges, like a tough exam or a problem with friends. Or consider Esther's story, where she used her voice to save her people and encourage them to speak up and make a difference. Seeing these connections between Bible stories and your own experiences can turn reading the Bible from a routine task into a source of inspiration and guidance.

Bible time can become one of the best parts of your day by choosing the correct Bible version, following a reading plan that fits you, using creative methods, and applying Bible lessons to your life. It's not just about reading an old book but discovering a guide of wisdom, comfort, and inspiration that's perfect for you as you grow up.

ACTIVITY - CHAPTER 1

Scan the QR code below to start the activity.

Chapter 2

Building Confidence and Self-Esteem

Have you ever seen a potter at work? With careful hands, they mold and shape clay, turning a simple lump into a beautiful piece of art. Just like the potter shapes his creation, God shapes you—crafting you with purpose, designing you uniquely, and loving you deeply. This chapter is about finding confidence in knowing you are God's masterpiece, wonderfully made and cherished. We'll explore how to see yourself the way God sees you and appreciate the unique beauty and purpose He has given you.

2.1 God's Masterpiece: Finding Confidence in Being God's Creation

Emphasize Divine Craftsmanship

Imagine God displaying you as a work of art in His gallery, thoughtfully choosing and lovingly placing every detail of who you are. Ephesians 2:10 says, **"For we are God's handiwork, created in Christ Jesus to do good works, which God prepared in advance for us to do."** This verse isn't just a nice thought; it's a powerful reminder of your worth. You are made with intention and purpose, just like an artist carefully plans every brushstroke. Understanding this can change how you see yourself and your abilities, giving you a strong sense of confidence that comes not from what the world says but from knowing that God values you deeply.

Illustrate with Creation Imagery

To understand what it means to be God's masterpiece, let's think about how the beauty of nature is like your own unique qualities. Think about the beauty of a sunset, the vastness of the ocean, or the delicate design of a butterfly's wings—each part of nature is unique and has a purpose. In the same way, your qualities and characteristics add something unique to the world around you. Maybe it's your contagious laugh that brightens someone's day, your sharp mind that solves problems, or your gentle spirit that brings calm in challenging situations—each trait you have is like a piece of the beautiful puzzle of life. These connections can help you see your value and purpose more clearly.

"Your smile will brighten the day for you're unique"

Self-reflection Exercises

To better appreciate your unique qualities, try self-reflection activities to help you see how you reflect God's craftsmanship. Set aside time each week to write down things you like about yourself. These can be physical traits, talents, or parts of your character. For each quality, think about how it has made a positive difference for others or brought you happiness. For example, if you're a natural leader, remember when you guided a group successfully. Connecting your qualities to positive outcomes can boost your self-esteem and help you see yourself the way God does—valuable and capable.

Counter Negative Self-Perceptions

Learning how to replace negative thoughts with the truth of God's word is essential in a world where it's easy to focus on your flaws. When you catch yourself thinking you're not good enough, remember Psalm 139:14: **"I praise you because I am fearfully and wonderfully made."** Use this verse to remind yourself of your worth as God's creation. You could also list Bible verses about God's love and plans for you. Whenever you feel down, read these verses to remind yourself of your unique place in the world and how much God values you.

By embracing these truths and practices, you begin to see yourself as God sees you—a precious and purposeful creation capable of great things. As we continue to explore ways to build confidence and self-esteem, remember that every step you take is a step toward seeing the full beauty and worth of who you are through the eyes of the One who made you.

2.2 Overcoming Comparison: How to Stop Comparing Yourself to Others

In a world where social media often shows a picture-perfect life, it's easy to fall into the comparison trap. Seeing posts of perfect vacations, significant achievements, and flawless looks can make you feel like everyone else has it better. But remember, these posts are just tiny, sometimes exaggerated, snapshots of reality. In this part of our journey together, we'll learn how to notice when we're most likely to compare ourselves to others and how to shift our focus to appreciate our unique paths and blessings.

Identifying Comparison Triggers

The first step to overcoming the habit of comparing yourself to others is knowing when and where you tend to do it. For many of us, social media is a big trigger. It's easy to see someone else's highlight reel and feel like your life doesn't measure up. Pay attention to how you feel during and after using social media. Do you feel less than, jealous, or unhappy with your achievements or looks? These feelings indicate that it's time to take a step back and consider how social media affects your self-esteem.

Another trigger can be when you feel pressured to look or act a certain way, like at school, on a sports team, or in a group of friends. Recognizing these triggers helps you make better choices to protect your self-esteem, like limiting your time on social media or changing how you think about what you see.

"Avoid comparison for it makes you feel sad"

Biblical Teachings About Individuality

The Bible shares many stories about the value of being ourselves and the dangers of comparing ourselves to others. Take Mary and Martha, two sisters who loved Jesus but showed it differently. In Luke 10:38-42, Martha is busy preparing everything, while Mary sits at Jesus' feet and listens to Him. When Martha complains that Mary isn't helping, Jesus gently reminds her that Mary has chosen what is better. This story shows that each of us has a unique role, and what is suitable for one person is only sometimes right for another. Like

Mary and Martha, God calls you to follow your path and do what fulfills you without comparing yourself to others.

Practical Steps to Reduce Comparison

A great way to move your focus from comparing yourself to others to focusing on your growth is through gratitude journaling. This practice means regularly writing down things you're thankful for. It could be simple blessings, things you've achieved, qualities you like about yourself, or ways you've helped others. Over time, focusing on gratitude can change how you see things, helping you notice all the good in your life instead of what you think is missing. This habit boosts your mood and enables you to appreciate your unique journey and the many blessings.

Additionally, when you set personal goals that align with your interests and values, instead of trying to reach what someone else has achieved, you stay focused on your growth. These goals include improving a skill, learning something new, or strengthening friendships and family connections.

Encouraging Community Support

Surrounding yourself with a supportive community that celebrates individual successes without comparing is critical to overcoming the habit of comparison. Find friends and groups who lift each other, share successes joyfully, and meet challenges with encouragement and support. In these environments, it's easier to feel valued for who you are, not just for what you achieve compared to others.

Participating in community service or group activities focusing on working together rather than competing can also help you appreciate everyone's contributions. These experiences remind you that everyone has something valuable to offer and that our differences and unique strengths make our communities more robust and vibrant.

By recognizing and addressing what triggers you to compare, embracing your unique self as God made you, practicing gratitude, setting personal goals, and building supportive relationships, you can start to break free from the trap of comparison. This change boosts your self-esteem and happiness and helps you celebrate others' blessings and successes without feeling less about yourself. As we continue exploring ways to build confidence and self-esteem, remember that each step you take brings you closer to fully appreciating and loving the unique and wonderful person you are, created with purpose and deeply loved by God.

2.3 The Power of Positive Self-Talk: Affirmations That Lift You Up

Teach the Power of Words

Think about the last time someone said something encouraging to you. Maybe it was a teacher who noticed your hard work or a friend who complimented your new hairstyle. How did those words make you feel lighter, happier, and more confident? Now, imagine giving yourself that same positive boost every day. That's the power of positive self-talk and affirmations.

Proverbs 18:21 in the Bible highlights the power of words: **"Death and life are in the power of the tongue."** This verse reminds us that words can significantly impact positively or negatively.

When you speak kindly to yourself and focus on your worth and strengths, you bring positivity and growth into your life. By making positive self-talk a habit, you improve your mood and build strength against negative thoughts and comments. It's like planting seeds of positivity that grow into a beautiful garden of self-confidence and joy.

Develop a List of Affirmations

Affirmations are positive statements that help you challenge and overcome negative thoughts and feelings. You see positive changes when you repeat them often and believe in them. For example, saying affirmations like "God loves me" or "I am created with a purpose" helps you align your thoughts with God's truth about who you are. Here's a simple list of biblical affirmations to get you started:

- **"I am fearfully and wonderfully made."** (Psalm 139:14)
- **"I can do all things through Christ who strengthens me."** (Philippians 4:13)
- **"God chooses me, holy and dearly loved."** (Colossians 3:12)
- **"God has not given me a spirit of fear, but of power, love, and a sound mind."** (II Timothy 1:7)
- **"I am the head and not the tail; I am above only, and not beneath."** (Deuteronomy 28:13)

Start and end your day by saying these affirmations out loud. As you do, imagine them sinking into your heart and taking root. Over time, these truths will replace any lies you've believed about yourself and become the soundtrack of your daily life, reminding you of God's love and true worth.

Create an Affirmation Craft

To make these affirmations a visible part of your daily life, let's dive into a fun DIY activity and create your affirmation cards! Here's what you'll need:

1. Card stock or heavy paper, colorful markers, stickers, and any other decorations you like.
2. Cut the card stock into small, portable cards.
3. On each card, write one affirmation in big, cheerful letters.
4. Decorate them with markers and stickers to make them bright and personal—something that makes you smile whenever you see them.

Once you finish, place the cards in spots where you will see them often, like on your bathroom mirror, study desk, or inside your school locker. Every time you visit your affirmation cards, take a moment to read them out loud and remind yourself of the powerful truths they hold. These visual reminders will give you little boosts of encouragement throughout your day.

"Say affirmative things to yourself"

Role-Play Scenarios

Let's role-play a few situations where negative self-talk usually takes over and see how to turn those thoughts around with positive affirmations. Imagine you just got a lower grade on a math test than expected. You might initially think, "I'm just not good at math." At this moment, pause, take a deep breath, and replace that thought with an affirmation such as, **"I am capable of learning and growing in every area, including math."** Or you're nervous about trying out for the school play. Instead of thinking, "I'm probably going to mess up," try saying, **"I am brave, and God gives me strength, no matter what happens."** By practicing this shift in everyday situations, you train your mind to choose positivity and resilience, changing your inner story to hope and encouragement.

Through these practices and changing how you talk to yourself, you can develop a more positive outlook on life, a stronger sense of self-worth, and a closer connection with God, who always speaks words of life and love into your heart.

2.4 Handling Criticism Gracefully: Learning From Others While Staying Strong

Imagine you've just shared a project you worked hard on with your class, but your teacher gives you harsh feedback instead of the praise you hoped for. Or you tried out for the lead role in the school play, and a friend said you probably wouldn't get the part. Moments like these can be challenging when you face criticism. But here's the good news: handling criticism can help you grow and improve. Let's explore how you can handle criticism with grace and strength, learning from it without letting it dim your shine.

Differentiate Constructive and Destructive Criticism

First, knowing the difference between constructive and destructive criticism is essential. Constructive criticism, like a coach giving you tips, helps you improve and grow. On the other hand, destructive criticism is like someone booing from the stands without any reason; it's often just hurtful. In the Bible, we see examples of helpful advice, like when Nathan, the prophet, spoke to King David about his mistake with Bathsheba (II Samuel 12). Nathan spoke directly but respectfully, intending to bring about positive change. This example demonstrates how wise advice comes with good intentions and a respectful tone. When you get feedback, ask yourself, "Is this meant to help me improve? Is it given kindly and respectfully?" If the answer is yes, it's constructive criticism.

Biblical Responses to Criticism

When facing criticism, seeing how Jesus responded to His critics is helpful. Even when faced with harsh criticism and direct attacks, He always answered with wisdom and calm. For instance, when the Pharisees criticized Jesus for healing on the Sabbath, He responded with a question highlighting their hypocrisy (Luke 14:3-4). This example teaches that responding to criticism with a calm, thoughtful question can sometimes clarify misunderstandings and reduce tension. It's also a good reminder that you don't have to accept criticism silently; you can stand up for yourself in a respectful way that keeps the conversation positive.

"Don't look sad because you're criticized"

Emotional Resilience Techniques

Criticism can hurt, and initially, it's natural to feel upset or defensive. That's when emotional resilience becomes essential—the ability to recover from those negative feelings. Techniques like deep breathing can be beneficial. When you feel overwhelmed by criticism, try taking a few deep breaths:

- Breathe in slowly through your nose.
- Hold it for a few seconds.
- Breathe out through your mouth.

This simple exercise can help calm your mind and give you a moment to think.

Prayer is another powerful tool. Share your feelings with God and ask for His peace and wisdom. Remember, Philippians 4:6-7 encourages us **not to be anxious but to bring our requests to God, and His peace will protect our hearts and minds.**

Encourage Seeking Clarification

Sometimes, criticism must be clarified, which can be confusing and frustrating. If you're unsure about the feedback you've received, don't be afraid to ask for clarification. You could say, "Can you explain what you mean by that?" or, "Can you give me an example?" Asking for specifics can help you understand the feedback better and show the person giving it that you're genuinely interested in improving. This approach enables you to learn more effectively and turns criticism into a constructive conversation, creating more opportunities for growth and development.

Handling criticism is a skill that will help you throughout your life. By learning to tell the difference between helpful and hurtful feedback, responding wisely, building your emotional strength, and asking for clarification, you can turn potentially discouraging experiences into opportunities for personal growth and greater self-confidence. Remember, every piece of feedback is a chance to learn something new about yourself and the world around you.

2.5 Celebrating Small Victories: Recognizing Your Achievements

Have you ever noticed how good it feels to cross something off your to-do list or get a high-five for a job well done? It's like a little spark of joy lights up inside you. Celebrating small victories isn't just about feeling good; it's about recognizing and appreciating every progress you make, no matter how small it seems. Celebrating these moments is essential because it builds momentum and keeps you motivated, especially when more considerable challenges come your way. Like a gardener who celebrates the first sprout in their garden, recognizing your growth helps build your confidence and self-esteem.

Let's talk about why it's essential to recognize your achievements. Every time you celebrate a win, no matter how small, you tell yourself, **"I can do this."** This positive thinking is crucial because it builds a mindset of confidence and determination, which helps you tackle more challenging tasks and goals. For example, if you've been struggling with math and score a little higher on a quiz, celebrating that improvement (instead of only focusing on not getting a perfect score) reinforces your ability to grow and learn. This shift in focus can change how you approach learning, making it less about fearing failure and more about enjoying the journey of getting better.

One effective way to track achievements is by maintaining a **"victory log"**. You could use a simple notebook, a section in a planner, or a digital document to record your daily or weekly wins. Maybe you helped a younger sibling with homework, shared an idea in class, or finally organized your desk the way you wanted—write it all down. Then, set aside time each week to review your victory log. This practice isn't just about self-praise; it's an opportunity to see how these small wins add up and contribute to achieving bigger goals. It's also an excellent way to know how you're using the gifts God has given you in both big and small ways.

"Celebrate small victories"

The Bible also shows us how celebrating achievements is linked to gratitude to God. For example, when King David brought the Ark of the Covenant to Jerusalem, the people celebrated with music, dancing, and offerings (II Samuel 6). This celebration was not only about the ark's arrival but also a way to express gratitude to God for His continuous faithfulness and guidance.

Similarly, when you achieve something—like improving a skill or overcoming a personal challenge—it's a chance to thank God for His guidance and strength. Recognizing that your abilities and opportunities are blessings helps cultivate a grateful heart, which the Bible teaches is critical to living a fulfilling life with God.

Connecting your celebrations to gratitude doesn't just make you appreciate your achievements more; it also strengthens your relationship with God. Each small victory becomes a reminder of His grace and a chance to thank Him for helping you grow. Whether celebrating a good grade, a stronger friendship, or another day of working toward your goals, remember to thank God for being with you every step of the way. Practicing gratitude deepens your faith and keeps you grounded in God's love and care, reminding you that every good thing comes from Him.

As you face challenges and celebrate victories, remember that each small win is like a brushstroke in the masterpiece God is creating in your life. Your growth is a beautiful process that deserves recognition and celebration—not just in big moments but in everyday triumphs that keep you moving forward.

2.6 Made for a Purpose: Discovering Your God-Given Talents and Abilities

Have you ever wondered what makes you uniquely you? What do you do that makes you feel alive and happy? Maybe it's drawing, solving math problems, leading a group, or making people laugh—we have unique talents and abilities. These aren't just random; they are gifts from God, woven into who you are, meant to be nurtured and shared. This part of your book is about discovering these gifts, developing them, and using them to make a difference in the world around you.

Identify Personal Talents

Let's start by discovering what your talents are. Think about the activities you enjoy, the things people often ask you to help with, or the subjects you learn quickly. These can be clues to your God-given talents. You may be a natural at public speaking, have a knack for understanding technology, or are the friend everyone turns to for advice. To help you determine your talents, try this exercise: list five activities you love doing and five skills people often compliment you on. Look for overlaps—your talents usually shine in these areas. Recognizing your abilities is the first step in embracing your unique role in God's story.

Encourage Skill Development

Once you've identified your talents, developing them is next. Think of your abilities as seeds that God has planted in you—seeds that need water, sunlight, and care to grow. You can nurture your talents through practice, which helps you get better and build confidence. For example, consider taking classes or practicing if you're talented in art. If you're a good speaker, look for chances to speak in front of others, like at church or school events.

Finding a mentor can also be incredibly helpful. A mentor who shares your talent can give you guidance, encouragement, and feedback, which are essential for your growth. Remember to include prayer in this process, asking God to help you develop your talents and use them in the way He wants. This way, you can beautifully take care of the gifts you've been given and make the most of them.

Connect Talents to Purpose

Your talents aren't just for you to enjoy; they're tools you can use to bless others and play your part in God's plan. Each talent you have can be a way to serve and help in your community and church. For example, if you're good at organizing, you could help coordinate volunteer events. If you're artistic, consider using your skills to brighten local community centers or teach art classes to younger children. By using your talents to serve others, you bring joy to those around you and find a more profound sense of purpose and fulfillment.

Inspiring Stories of Purpose

The Bible contains stories about young people who used their talents for a greater purpose. Take Timothy, for example. He was a young man with a talent for leadership and teaching. With guidance from Paul, he grew into a significant leader in the early church, using his abilities to spread the gospel and strengthen believers. Then there's Esther, a young woman who used her courage and position to save her people. These stories aren't just old tales; they remind us that God can use your talents for essential purposes, regardless of age.

As you continue to explore and develop your talents, remember that God uniquely equips you to make a difference in the world. Your talents are part of His divine plan, and when you use them to help others, you step into your full potential. Discovering and using your talents isn't just about feeling good—it's about contributing to something bigger and improving the world, one small act at a time.

As we finish this chapter on building confidence and self-esteem, remember that recognizing your worth, overcoming comparison, speaking kindly to yourself, handling criticism well, and celebrating your victories are all essential steps to seeing yourself as God sees you. Each step you take matters—not just in building your self-esteem but preparing you for the exciting life God has planned for you. In the next chapter, we'll explore how these parts of personal growth are essential for developing and maintaining healthy relationships.

ACTIVITY - CHAPTER 2

Scan the QR code to start the activity.

Hey there, amazing reader!
Review Us!
Loving the book so far? We'd love to hear your thoughts! Take a quick break to leave a review by scanning the QR code or click the link below. Your feedback can inspire other young girls on their journey. Thank you!

Chapter 3

Navigating Relationships

"**Have you ever wondered what makes a friendship shine?** It's like having a secret recipe where every ingredient matters—trust, laughter, shared moments, and sometimes, a few tears. As you grow and change, so do your relationships. This chapter is all about helping you navigate the rewarding yet sometimes complex world of friendships. Whether making new friends, deepening existing bonds, or even getting through disagreements, learning how to handle these relationships can make a big difference in your life and faith journey. So, are you ready to explore what makes your friendships special?"

3.1 Choosing Friends Wisely: What the Bible Says About Friendship

"Have friends with great qualities"

Friendship is one of life's greatest joys and blessings. Consider David and Jonathan, whose friendship was so strong that Jonathan helped David escape from his father, King Saul, who wanted to harm David. Their story, found in the books of I and II Samuel, shows us the power of a true friend—someone who loves selflessly and stands by you even when it's difficult for them. This is a reason to be grateful for the friends we have in our lives.

Another beautiful example is Ruth and Naomi from the book of Ruth. Even after losing her husband, Ruth's loyalty to her mother-in-law, Naomi, is a powerful example of steadfast love and commitment. She famously told Naomi, "**Where you go, I will go, and where you stay, I will stay. Your people will be my people, and your God my God.**" These stories aren't just old tales; they offer timeless lessons about what makes friendships deep and lasting.

When choosing friends, looking for qualities that help build a healthy and positive relationship is essential. Proverbs 27:17 says, "**As iron sharpens iron, so one person sharpens another.**" This verse reminds us that good friends help us grow in character and faith. So, what does this look like in real life? A good friend is honest, even when it's tough. They are loyal, sticking with you through good times and bad. They share your values, especially when it comes to your faith. A friend who shares your commitment to following Jesus can encourage you when you're struggling and celebrate your successes in living out your faith.

However, not all friendships are good for us. It's essential to recognize the signs of unhealthy relationships. If a friendship consistently makes you feel drained, pressures you to compromise your values, or is filled with negativity, it might not be healthy for you or your spiritual growth. For instance, if a friend constantly criticizes your faith or tries to persuade you to do things that go against your beliefs, it's a sign that the friendship may not benefit your spiritual journey. It's okay to set boundaries in friendships or step back if a relationship affects your well-being or pulls you away from your values.

Prayer plays a crucial role in forming and maintaining healthy friendships. James 1:5 says, **"If any of you lacks wisdom, ask God, who gives it generously to all without finding fault, and He will provide it to you."** If you're unsure about a friendship, bring it to God in prayer. Ask Him for wisdom to know if the friendship is proper for you and how to handle it. This reassures us that we are never alone in our relationships. Praying for your friends is also essential; it supports them and strengthens the spiritual bond between you.

Navigating friendships isn't just about making good choices; it's about building a community that reflects the love and faithfulness we see in the Bible. As you think about your friendships and look to make new ones, remember that each friend can influence your life and faith. Choose wisely, care for your friendships, and always seek God's guidance in your relationships.

3.2 Dealing with Peer Pressure: Standing Firm in Your Faith

Do you ever feel like everyone around you is watching and waiting to see what you'll choose to do in a situation? It could be about wearing certain clothes, listening to specific music, or making choices that don't align with your values. This feeling often comes from peer pressure, which isn't just someone trying to get you to do something you don't want to; it's usually more subtle. In a religious context, peer pressure can manifest as friends or acquaintances encouraging you to engage in activities or behaviors that contradict your faith. It could be a group of friends deciding to skip church or prayer, and you feel left out if you don't join in. Peer pressure can sneak up on you in these quiet moments, making it hard to stay true to your beliefs and values.

The Bible story of Daniel provides one of the most empowering examples of resisting peer pressure. When Daniel arrived in Babylon, the king's officials pressured him to eat the king's food, but he resisted because it went against his dietary rules and commitment to God. Instead of giving in, Daniel suggested a test: he and his friends would eat only vegetables and drink water for ten days. After this period, Daniel and his friends looked healthier than those who ate the king's food. This story isn't just about food; it's about having the courage to stick to your beliefs, even when it might be easier to fit in. Daniel's faithfulness shows us that standing firm isn't just possible; it's rewarding. This empowers us to stand up for our beliefs, even under pressure.

When you face similar pressures, having practical ways to say no can be helpful—knowing what you believe and why makes it much easier to stand up for yourself. For example, if someone tries to pressure you into gossiping, and you value kindness, you could say, "I'm trying to focus on speaking kindly about others. Let's talk about something else." This way, you're not just saying no but also standing up for your beliefs positively. Another strategy is to suggest an alternative. If your friends want to watch a movie that makes you uncomfortable, you could say, "I heard another movie is great! How about we watch that instead?" Offering another option keeps things light and cheerful while staying true to your principles.

A big part of resisting peer pressure is having confidence in your beliefs. Confidence doesn't mean you're always right; it means trusting the values you've chosen to guide your life. Building this kind of confidence starts with exploring and understanding your faith. The more you learn about your beliefs, the more intensely you can stand when others challenge them. Activities like Bible study, prayer, and talking with trusted adults can deepen your understanding and strengthen your resolve. Remember, every time you stand firm, you're not just saying no to peer pressure; you're saying yes to the person you want to be.

Resisting peer pressure isn't just about avoiding negative influences but actively shaping who you are through your everyday choices. Every time you align with your faith, you reinforce your identity and goals. These choices aren't just challenges; they're chances to show your commitment to your values and your chosen path, even when it's the road less traveled. As you face different pressures from peers, remember you shape the foundation of your character, guiding you to become the person you are destined to become.

3.3 The Bond of Family: Strengthening Family Ties Through Faith

When you think about your family, you probably picture the people who are always there for you—cheering you on at soccer games, helping with homework, and being by your side. Your family can also be an excellent spiritual support, helping you grow in faith and strengthening your bonds with each other and God. It's like weaving a more substantial thread that holds everything together, especially during tough times.

Think about how families in the Bible supported each other in faith. For example, Timothy from the New Testament was known for his faith, which he first learned from his grandmother, Lois, and his mother, Eunice (II Timothy 1:5). This shows us that faith can be a beautiful legacy passed down through family members, enriching each generation. How can you create a spiritually supportive environment in your own family? **Start with shared faith practices.** Set aside time each week to study the Bible together, discuss its teachings, and make time for everyone to share their thoughts and learn from each other. It doesn't have to be long or formal; consistency and openness are key. Praying together during family devotions or before bedtime can also build a sense of unity and trust, reminding everyone that your family is a team working together under God's guidance.

But what if your family members have different opinions or beliefs? That's quite common, especially as everyone ages and explores their paths. Dealing with these differences requires patience and love, which are fruits of the Spirit (Galatians 5:22-23). When discussions about faith or life choices arise, approach them with understanding rather than judgment. For example, if a family member doubts something you believe in, use this as a chance to have an open conversation, not a debate. Ask questions like, **"What makes you feel that way?"** or **"Can I share why I believe differently?"** These questions show respect for others' feelings and encourage healthy, respectful conversations that can lead to greater understanding.

Activities to Enhance Family Bonds

"Build a strong relationship with your family"

Building stronger family bonds can also include fun activities that everyone enjoys. Try organizing a weekly family devotional night where each person shares something—a favorite Bible verse, a song, or a personal story. Doing this makes everyone feel involved and valued. Another great idea is to plan a family service project. Pick a cause that matters to you, like **volunteering at a local food bank** or **organizing a community clean-up.** Working together on a project creates beautiful memories and teaches important lessons in kindness and teamwork.

Encouraging Open Communication

Open communication is the foundation of a healthy family relationship. It means feeling safe to express your thoughts and feelings without fear of being dismissed or criticized. To create this kind of environment, **be a good listener**. When someone is speaking, could you give them your full attention? Show that you're interested in what they're saying by nodding or using phrases like, "I see," or, "That sounds interesting; tell me more." Avoid rushing to give advice or make judgments. Sometimes, people need to feel heard and understood. Also, be open to sharing your feelings. Use "I" statements, like "I feel" or "I think," which can help prevent others from feeling defensive. This open, respectful communication approach helps everyone feel more connected and supported.

As you continue to bring faith into your family life, remember that every family is unique; there isn't a one-size-fits-all approach. What works for one family might not work for another. The key is to **keep love, respect, and faith at the center**, finding practices that bring out the best in everyone and help you grow together, not just as a family but as a small community of faith navigating life together. Whether through shared prayers, exploring Scripture, or serving others, every step you take to strengthen family bonds can lead to a more prosperous, more fulfilling faith journey for everyone.

3.4 Resolving Conflicts: A Godly Approach to Disagreements

Have you ever argued about a misunderstanding with a sibling who gets the remote or with a friend? It's normal to have disagreements from time to time. After all, we all have different thoughts, opinions, and feelings. What matters is how we handle these conflicts. The Bible contains stories about resolving conflicts, showing that even prophets and apostles disagreed. But they dealt with these situations with grace and wisdom, offering valuable lessons on resolving disputes in ways that make relationships stronger instead of weaker.

Let's look at how biblical teachings can help us resolve disputes. Ephesians 4:15 encourages us to speak the truth in love, a crucial first step in resolving conflict. Speaking the truth in love involves being honest about your feelings and thoughts while remaining respectful and mindful of others' emotions. Try to balance expressing your needs with listening to what others say. For example, if you're upset because your friend forgot to save you a seat at lunch, instead of saying, "You always ignore me!" you could try, "I felt left out when there wasn't a seat for me. Let's find a way to ensure it doesn't happen again." This approach opens a conversation and helps your friend understand your feelings without criticism.

Forgiveness is also crucial in resolving conflicts. Jesus taught us a lot about forgiveness and its importance in our relationships. In Matthew 18:21-22, Peter asks Jesus how many times he should forgive someone who wrongs him, suggesting, "Up to seven times?" Jesus replies, **"Not seven times, but seventy-seven times,"** showing that forgiveness should be endless. Holding onto anger or resentment after a disagreement only causes more hurt, while forgiveness leads to healing and reconciliation. It's not about keeping track or waiting for the other person to apologize first; it's about letting go of bitterness to make room for peace and restoring your relationship.

Role-Play Scenarios

Consider a few everyday situations you might encounter when implementing these principles.

Situation: Your sibling borrows your favorite sweater without asking and spills something on it, making you worry that it will be permanently stained.

Response: Instead of getting angry immediately, take a few deep breaths to calm down. Then, talk to your sibling and explain calmly, "I'm distraught because that sweater is special to me, and now it's stained. I wish you had asked me before borrowing it." Discuss ways to fix the situation, like getting the sweater cleaned. Share your forgiveness and talk about how to avoid similar situations in the future.

***

Situation: A classmate spreads a rumor about you that isn't true.

Response: Find a private moment to talk to your classmate. You might say, "I heard a rumor going around, and it hurt my feelings because it's not true. Can we talk about how this happened?" Listen to their story, express how it made you feel, and find ways to clear up the misunderstanding. Offer forgiveness and emphasize that you want to move past it and restore your friendship.

***

Situation: Your friend is consistently late when you make plans, and it's starting to upset you because you set time aside and look forward to it.

Response: Bring up the issue directly but kindly. Say something like, "I feel like my time isn't valued when you're late. Can we work on this?" Discuss why they might be late and find ways to prevent it from happening again. Express your willingness to forgive past instances and hope that things will improve.

***

Handling conflicts isn't just about solving problems—it's about growing in love, understanding, and patience with those around you. Every time you face a disagreement, remember it's an opportunity to practice the godly virtues of **truthfulness, forgiveness, and love**, building stronger, more lasting relationships that reflect the love of Christ.

3.5 Be a Good Friend: Support Others with Compassion

Friendship is like a garden; it flourishes with care, attention, and heart. One of the best parts of friendship is supporting and uplifting each other, especially during tough times. It's essential to cultivate empathy—the ability to understand and share your friends' feelings—the ability to understand and share your friends' feelings. Empathy goes beyond feeling sorry for someone; it means putting yourself in your friend's shoes, feeling what they feel, and offering the support they need. For example, if your friend failed a test, empathy is more than saying, "That's too bad." It means sitting with them and saying, "I know how hard you studied, and I'm sorry about the result. How can I help you prepare next time?"

Developing empathy can change how you interact with friends and help you build deeper connections. Start by really listening when your friends talk about their feelings or problems. Instead of thinking about what to say next or how it relates to your experiences, focus entirely on their words and emotions.

Active listening helps you understand their perspective better and shows that you genuinely care about their feelings. Another way to build empathy is by being open about your own emotions. Sharing your feelings can encourage your friends to share, creating a deeper understanding and stronger bond.

"Have friends who you can share your feeling with"

Supporting friends also involves doing specific things that show you care. Small gestures can have a significant impact, such as sending a thoughtful text to a friend going through a tough time or spending time with them doing something fun to lift their spirits. Encouragement is another powerful way to support your friends. Remind them of their strengths and past successes when they feel unsure or afraid. For example, if a friend is nervous about an upcoming dance performance, remind her of the last time she performed beautifully on stage. These positive reminders can boost her confidence and ease her anxiety.

The Bible gives us excellent examples of supportive friendships. Consider the story of Job and his friends. When disaster struck Job, his friends did something remarkable: they sat with him in silence for seven days, sharing in his suffering without saying a word (Job 2:13). This act of just being present and sharing in the sorrow is a powerful example of empathy and support, even though they later made mistakes by wrongly accusing Job. This story shows that sometimes, the best way to support a friend is simply by offering silent support before jumping to solutions or judgments.

Lastly, practicing **kindness and selflessness** benefits those you help and enriches your life. Altruism—caring about others without expecting anything in return—is a principle deeply rooted in Christian teachings. Jesus said, **"It is more blessed to give than to receive"** (Acts 20:35). Doing kind things without expecting anything back can make your life more joyful and fulfilling. Acts of kindness can include:

- Volunteering together at a community center.
- Helping a friend with their homework.
- Cheering a friend on at a competition.

These acts build a foundation of generosity and care in your friendships, making them stronger and more resilient during tough times.

By embracing empathy, actively listening, offering encouragement, and practicing kindness, you can build friendships that are not only fulfilling but also reflect the love and compassion that are central to Christian values. As you continue to support your friends with compassion, you'll find that these relationships bring you deep joy and satisfaction, echoing the biblical proverb, **"A friend loves at all times, and a brother is born for a time of adversity"** (Proverbs 17:17).

3.6 Reaching Out: Making New Friends and Building Community

Stepping into a room full of strangers or trying to join a new group can feel like standing at the edge of a diving board for the first time—anticipation, nervousness, and excitement all rolled into one. Feeling anxious about making new friends is natural, especially if you're more reserved or if past experiences have made you cautious. But remember, God often calls us to step out of our comfort zones, even when making new friends. Consider when God called Abraham to leave his homeland and go to a new place that He would show him (Genesis 12:1). He stepped into the unknown, trusting God's promise, and his leap of faith led to future blessings. While making new friends isn't the same as moving to a new country, it does require a similar trust in God's plan for your social life.

First, let's address common fears and anxieties about meeting new people. Feeling shy or nervous is perfectly okay. Turning to Scripture can encourage. Isaiah 41:10 says, **"So do not fear, for I am with you; do not be dismayed, for I am your God. I will strengthen and help you and uphold you with my righteous right hand."** Remembering that God is with you can give you the courage to say hello first, join a new club, or sit with someone new at lunch. It can also help to set small, manageable goals, like introducing yourself to one new person a week or joining a group that meets regularly, such as a church youth group or a school club that interests you.

Finding the right community is crucial for your personal and spiritual growth. When looking for groups or clubs to join, consider what matters most. What are your passions and values?

Groups that match your interests in music, sports, or books are great, but consider how they align with your values. A community that uplifts, supports, and encourages each other in faith can strengthen your own beliefs and provide valuable support. Acts 2:46-47 describes the early Christians who spent time together, ate together, and praised God, finding favor with all people. This kind of supportive community can significantly enrich your faith journey.

"Meet new friends that will make you grow"

Let's talk about expanding your circle of friends. Being active in different communities helps you meet new people, understand other perspectives, and build a diverse network of relationships. You can do this by volunteering for causes you care about, joining clubs with various activities, or participating in community events. Each of these settings offers unique opportunities to connect with people who share your interests and to learn new ideas and experiences. As you meet new people, remember that friendships take time to grow. Be patient with yourself and others, and let your relationships develop naturally.

Maintaining friendships requires **effort and commitment**, much like tending a garden. Regular communication is essential—checking in with each other and being there for important moments. Mutual respect is vital; respecting others' opinions, boundaries, and differences helps create a strong foundation for lasting friendships. Remember, Proverbs 17:17 says, **"A friend loves at all times, and a brother is born for adversity."** True friends stand by you through life's ups and downs, always ready to offer encouragement, a listening ear, or a shoulder to lean on.

As you reach out to make new friends and build your community, remember that each person you meet can teach you something valuable. Embrace the opportunity to expand your horizons, learn from others, and grow in empathy and understanding. Through these new connections, you're not just building a network of friends but also creating a richer, more colorful tapestry of life that reflects the diversity and beauty of God's creation.

As we finish this chapter on navigating relationships, remember the key points we've covered about choosing friends wisely, dealing with peer pressure, strengthening family bonds, resolving conflicts, and being a good friend. Your interactions with others offer a chance to reflect Christ's love and grow in patience and understanding. As we move to the next chapter, we'll explore how you can turn life's challenges into opportunities for growth and learning, reminding you that every experience actively shapes who you are becoming.

ACTIVITY - CHAPTER 3

Scan the QR code to start the activity.

Chapter 4

Dealing with Challenges

Life is a tricky puzzle that throws in pieces you never expected. Sometimes, those pieces need to fit somewhere, which can be frustrating. Have you ever had a day where nothing seemed to go your way? Maybe you were looking forward to a fun day at the park, but it rained, or you were excited about a test you studied hard for but didn't get the grade you hoped for. It's normal to feel upset or disappointed in those moments. But here's the exciting part: these are the moments when you learn the most about God's incredible plans for you!

4.1 When Things Don't Go My Way: Understanding God's Plan

Acknowledge Disappointment

It's important to know that feeling disappointed doesn't mean you lack faith or are not a good Christian. It just means you're human! Everyone feels disappointed sometimes. What you do with that feeling can make all the difference. When things don't go as planned, feeling sad, crying, or even angry is okay. God understands these feelings—He created us with emotions, after all. He wants you to come to Him with those feelings. Just like you'd run to a parent or a friend for advice, God wants you to bring your disappointment to Him. He's there to listen, comfort, and guide you through those tough times, providing a comforting presence and a guiding light amid disappointment.

"God understands your feelings because He created us with emotions"

Introducing the Concept of God's Sovereignty

But why do disappointing things happen if God is in control? To answer this, we need to understand the concept of God's sovereignty. It's a big word, but it means that God has a plan for everything, and His ways are higher than ours. This means that even when things go wrong—like when you don't make the team or a friend lets you down—God can use those situations for a good purpose, even if it doesn't make sense to you right now. Trust that He's working for your good, even in the tough times.

Sharing Biblical Stories of Unexpected Outcomes

Consider Joseph's story in the Bible—it's a perfect example. Joseph was sold into slavery by his brothers, which was a terrible situation. However, those unfortunate events eventually led to Joseph becoming a leader in Egypt, where he was able to save his family during a famine. From being a slave to becoming a savior for his people, Joseph's journey shows that God can turn even the worst situations into something unique over time. Isn't it incredible to think God can take our most challenging moments and turn them into something good?

Trust in God

So, how do you keep trusting God's plan, especially when things seem wrong? First, turn to God through prayer. Tell Him how you feel and ask Him to help you see His hand in your situation. Remember, God's timing is not always our timing, and His ways are not always our ways. Journaling about God's faithfulness can also be a powerful reminder that He is always working in your life, even when you don't see it. Write down times when you've seen God answer a prayer or help you in a tough situation. When you face new challenges, you can remember how God helped you. Don't hesitate to talk to trusted adults like parents, pastors, or youth leaders. They can offer wisdom, pray with you, and help you understand how to trust God's plan for your life.

Navigating disappointment isn't easy, but with God's help, you can view challenges as opportunities to grow closer to Him and strengthen your faith. Remember, you're not walking your path alone—God is with you every step of the way, turning challenges into victories in the fantastic story He's writing for your life. Trust that even when things seem harsh, He's shaping you into someone strong, faithful, and hopeful.

4.2 Bullying: Finding Strength and Solace in Scripture

Bullying is a tough challenge many people face, and understanding it is the first step in dealing with it effectively. Bullying can show up in many forms: physical, like hitting or damaging someone's belongings; verbal, like name-calling or insults; and online, through social media, which is known as cyberbullying. Bullying can profoundly affect how you feel about yourself and the world around you. It can make you feel scared, lonely, or unsure of yourself. Remember, these feelings are valid. Bullying isn't just about the physical or emotional pain it causes; it also impacts your spirit and can shake your faith.

In these moments, Scripture offers profound comfort and strength. Psalm 34:18 says, **"The Lord is close to the brokenhearted and saves those who are crushed in spirit."** This verse is a powerful reminder that God is with you during the most challenging times, ready to offer comfort and help. When you feel hurt or scared because of bullying, remember this promise—God is closer than you might think, prepared to heal your heart and restore your spirit. The words of Scripture are not just words. They are a source of power and resilience that can help you stand firm in the face of bullying.

Knowing how to respond to bullying is essential. One effective way is to practice assertive responses. Being assertive means expressing your feelings clearly and calmly without being aggressive. For instance, when someone says something hurtful, you might reply, "I didn't appreciate that comment, and I won't accept being spoken to like that." It's also important to know when to ask for help from an adult, like a teacher, counselor, or parent. Standing up to bullying sometimes means getting support when the situation feels too much to handle alone. You can practice these scenarios with someone you trust, like a family member or friend, to help you prepare for real-life situations. Practicing what to say and do can make you feel more confident standing up for yourself and others.

Forgiveness is another powerful way to respond to bullying, even though it can be one of the hardest. Forgiving someone who has hurt you doesn't mean you think what they did was okay. Instead, it means letting go of anger and hurt so those feelings don't continue harming you. Matthew 6:14-15 says, **"For if you forgive other people when they sin against you, your heavenly Father will also forgive you."** Forgiveness can free your heart from bitterness and help healing begin. It's a step toward peace and can change how you see yourself and the situation. It's a powerful tool that can empower you to rise above the hurt and find peace in your heart.

Remember, forgiveness is a personal process and might take time, but it's a powerful tool that God gives us to keep peace in our hearts and minds.

Dealing with bullying is never easy, but with God's word as your shield and His love guiding you, you can find strength and comfort. **Remember, no one has the right to make you feel less than who you are—a beloved child of God,** created with a purpose and worth far beyond what anyone can take away.

4.3 Handling School Stress: Strategies to Stay Calm and Focused

School sometimes feels like a juggling act, with all the homework, exams, projects, and trying to have a social life! It's normal to feel stressed occasionally, but the key is learning to manage it so it doesn't overwhelm you. Let's look at some strategies to help you stay calm and focused, even during super busy weeks.

First, identify the primary sources of stress you face in school. Everyday stressors include assignment deadlines, exam pressures, and daily homework. Then there are social pressures—fitting in, making and keeping friends, and participating in extracurricular activities. Recognizing your stressors is the first step in handling them. Once you know what triggers your stress, you can tackle each step.

Next up is a super **important skill—time management**. Managing your time well can significantly reduce stress and help you feel more in control of your day. Start by creating a study schedule that divides your week into manageable parts. Use a planner or a digital calendar to block time for homework, projects, fun activities, and rest. Prioritizing tasks is also crucial. Pick the top three tasks that need your attention each day and start with those. You'll have completed the most important tasks even if you don't finish everything. Also, don't let big projects overwhelm you—break them down into smaller steps. Outline what needs to be done and tackle each step individually. This approach makes big tasks more manageable and gives you a clear path.

Developing healthy study habits is another key to success. One great habit is taking regular breaks. Did you know your brain can only focus intensely for about 45-50 minutes at a time? After that, it needs a break to recharge. Try the Pomodoro Technique: **study for 25 minutes, then take a 5-minute break.** Do something different during your break—stretch, grab a snack, or step outside for a few minutes. These activities can refresh your mind and help you focus better when you return to studying. Setting specific goals for each study session also helps. Before you start, write down what you aim to accomplish, whether reading a set number of pages, completing a math worksheet, or reviewing notes. Having a clear goal keeps you focused and motivated.

"Take a 5 min break after 25 min of reading to get refreshed"

Finally, let's talk about relaxation techniques to manage stress effectively. Deep breathing exercises are a powerful way to reduce stress. Try this: breathe deeply through your nose, expand your belly, then slowly breathe out through your mouth. Repeat a few times and feel the tension leave your body. Prayer, meditation, and reading Scripture can also bring immense peace and focus. Spend a few minutes each day in prayer, sharing your worries with God and reflecting on His promises. Verses like Philippians 4:6-7 remind us not to be anxious but to present our concerns to God with gratitude, bringing comfort and refocusing our minds on what truly matters.

By identifying your stressors, managing your time wisely, developing healthy study habits, and using relaxation techniques, you can handle school challenges more calmly and focus. Remember, it's not about being perfect or doing everything at once; it's about finding what works for you and taking small steps each day to manage your stress and reach your goals.

4.4 Coping with Change: New Beginnings Through Faith

Change is as natural as the shifting seasons or how the moon waxes and wanes in the night sky. It's everywhere, from how your interests evolve to moving to a new school or welcoming a new family member. Despite its constancy, change often feels unsettling. It pushes you out of your comfort zone, shakes your routine, and sometimes makes you question your place and purpose. It's not unusual to feel uncomfortable; that's how we're wired. The brain loves predictability. When familiar patterns change, you might feel like you've walked into a room where all the furniture has been moved around. Everything is in a different place, and it takes time to reorient yourself.

But the Bible is rich with stories that show how change while challenging, can be a gateway to fulfilling God's plan for you. Think about Abraham. God asked him to leave his homeland, his family, and the life he knew to go to an unknown land. He stepped into vast change, not knowing where it would lead. That act of faith resulted in God blessing him and his descendants, making him a father of many nations. Then there's Paul, who experienced one of the most dramatic transformations in the Bible. From persecuting Christians to becoming one of Christ's most devoted apostles, Paul's life changed entirely after encountering Jesus on the road to Damascus. That change led to the spreading of the Gospel worldwide. Both stories involve significant change that leads to even greater purposes. They teach us that while change might be uncomfortable or scary, it can open doors to extraordinary opportunities and deeper faith.

When you face changes, big or small, you can take practical steps to handle them with faith and confidence. Staying connected with friends and family is vital. Just like a tree withstands strong winds with deep roots, being surrounded by loved ones provides stability and strength. These people know and care about you, offering comfort and advice when uncertain. Regular spiritual practices like prayer, Bible reading, and attending church provide comfort and guidance. These practices keep you connected to God, your ultimate source of peace and stability. They remind you that even when everything around you changes, God's love for you remains the same.

Setting new goals can help you feel in control of change rather than like it's controlling you. Your goals don't have to be huge; they can be as simple as making a new friend in class, learning a new skill, or deepening your understanding of a Bible passage. Goals provide a sense of direction and purpose, turning the uncertainty of change into a manageable action plan you're excited about. They can be like beacons of light guiding you through new experiences.

Finally, embracing the new opportunities that come with change can shift your perspective. Instead of seeing change as losing the familiar, see it as a chance to grow and learn new things about yourself and the world around you. Whether discovering a talent you didn't know you had or finding a new strength in your faith, change can be enriching. It's like turning over a new leaf and finding vibrant growth underneath. It invites you to expand your horizons, step out in faith, and trust that God is with you, leading you where you need to be.

Navigating change is about learning how to dance in the rain, understanding that it contributes to your growth, nurtures your spirit, and refreshes your path. With each change, you are shaped, molded, and prepared for the beautiful plans God has in store for you—plans that may require you to step out of the old and into the new with courage and faith.

4.5 Overcoming Fear and Anxiety: Trusting God in Uncertain Times

When you feel scared or anxious, it may seem like you're the only one struggling, but everyone faces those feelings at some point, especially during the tween years when so many things are changing. Fear of failing a test, anxiety about making new friends, or even the dread of trying something new—these feelings are common, but they don't have to overwhelm you. Instead, they can be stepping stones to deeper faith and trust in God.

The first step in managing fear and anxiety is understanding where they come from. Often, these feelings stem from the unknown—the "what ifs" that swirl in your mind about situations you can't predict or control. Fear of failure might make you anxious about handing in a project or trying out for a sports team, or maybe you're worried about not being good enough. Fear of rejection can make starting conversations at a new school seem daunting. Recognizing these triggers is critical because once you know what's causing your anxiety, you can address it with truth and faith.

"Read the bible to overcome your fears"

Scripture offers powerful reassurances for times when fear feels overwhelming. Isaiah 41:10 is a beautiful reminder: **"So do not fear, for I am with you; do not be dismayed, for I am your God. I will strengthen and help you and uphold you with my righteous right hand."** These words aren't just comforting; they are a promise from God that He is always with you, providing the strength and support you need. When anxiety tries to take hold, these truths can be an anchor, reminding you that you are not alone and are always secure in God's mighty hand.

Alongside leaning on God's word, there are practical tools to manage anxiety. Mindfulness is a helpful technique for focusing on the present moment instead of worrying about the past or future. Practicing mindfulness can be as simple as pausing for a minute, taking deep breaths, and paying attention to what you see, hear, and feel around you. This practice can calm your mind and bring you back to peace. Focusing on present blessings is another way to combat anxiety. Try keeping a gratitude journal where you write down things you're thankful for each day. Keeping this journal can shift your focus from worries to blessings, lifting your spirit and reminding you of the many good gifts God has placed in your life.

Another effective strategy is to create **a fear-to-faith plan**. Identify your fear, then write God's word about that situation. For instance, find scriptures about

God's guidance and companionship if you're scared about moving to a new school. Next, decide on a practical step to face that fear, like visiting the new school before the term starts or meeting a future classmate beforehand.

Finally, commit this plan to prayer, asking God to fill you with confidence and peace. When you turn a fear into a faith-building action, you manage your anxiety and strengthen your trust in God.

By understanding the roots of fear, soaking in the truths of Scripture, using practical anxiety-management techniques, and actively turning fear into moments of faith, you can navigate uncertain times with a heart anchored in God's peace. Remember, each step you take in overcoming fear is a step toward a deeper, more confident faith that knows and trusts the ever-present help of your loving Father. Keep moving forward, knowing God is with you, guiding you with His love and strength.

4.6 The Power of Forgiveness: Healing Broken Relationships Through Christ

Forgiveness sometimes feels like a tall mountain, especially when the hurt runs deep. But embracing forgiveness isn't just about making things suitable with someone else; it's about freeing your own heart from the weight of resentment and anger. It's a gift you give yourself, just as much as it's a gift you offer others. The Lord's Prayer includes a powerful line: "**Forgive us our debts, as we also have forgiven our debtors**" (Matthew 6:12). This isn't just a plea for God's forgiveness; it's a call to live out that same forgiveness in your life, showing that forgiveness is deeply connected to your own experience of divine forgiveness.

The Bible contains examples of forgiveness that restored relationships and transformed lives. Think of Joseph, who endured betrayal and suffering from his brothers but chose to forgive them—an act that led to the restoration of his family (Genesis 45). Even more compelling is the example of Jesus who, while dying on the cross, forgave those who crucified Him, saying, "**Father, forgive**

them, for they do not know what they are doing" (Luke 23:34). These acts of forgiveness are potent reminders that no situation is beyond the reach of grace and reconciliation.

There are practical steps you can take to forgive. First, **acknowledge the hurt.** It's okay to admit that you're hurt; recognizing and validating your feelings is a crucial step toward healing. Once you've acknowledged the hurt, make a conscious decision to forgive. Choosing to forgive doesn't mean denying the pain or pretending it didn't matter; it means deciding not to let that pain define or control your life anymore. This step might require you to ask God to soften your heart and give you the strength to forgive, especially when the hurt feels too heavy to let go of on your own.

The next step is to **express forgiveness**, which might look different depending on the situation. If it's safe and appropriate, expressing forgiveness could involve a conversation where you tell the person you forgive them. However, sometimes, forgiveness might not involve direct communication, especially if the relationship isn't safe or healthy. In that case, you might affirm forgiveness in your heart or prayer.

It's also essential to understand the difference between forgiveness and reconciliation. Forgiveness is a requirement, a command that frees you from bitterness. Reconciliation, however, depends on the situation. It involves restoring trust and returning to a close relationship, which might only sometimes be possible or wise if the other person's behavior has stayed the same. Forgiveness doesn't mean putting yourself back into a harmful or painful situation. It means letting go of the bitterness while taking wise steps to protect your heart and well-being.

"Learn how to forgive"

Embracing forgiveness is embracing freedom to heal, grow, and open your heart to the peace and joy God wants for you. As we conclude this chapter on dealing with challenges, remember that each hurdle—disappointment, bullying, stress, change, fear, or strained relationships—offers growth and renewal opportunities. Through each difficulty, lean more deeply into your faith, trust God's unfailing love and power, and extend that grace to others.

As we move into the next chapter, we'll continue exploring how each challenge can become a stepping stone, leading you closer to the person God has created you to be. Let's walk this path with open hearts to learn, forgive, and grow.

ACTIVITY - CHAPTER 4

Scan the QR code to start the activity.

Chapter 5

Growing in Faith

Did you ever start a hobby you were excited about, like painting or playing a new sport? At first, everything was new and a bit challenging, but as you kept at it, you began to see your skills grow and your confidence bloom.

Growing in faith is a lot like that. It starts with small, daily steps—moments spent with God, little prayers whispered in the night, and verses that stick with you throughout the day. Each small act is like a brushstroke on a canvas, gradually creating a beautiful picture of a life lived with God. Think about it: what small steps could you take today to grow closer to God? Let's explore how crafting personal time with God daily can be part of your foundation, helping you grow deeper in faith and more vital as you walk with Him.

5.1 Daily Devotions: Crafting Personal Time with God

Establishing Routine

Creating a daily devotional routine is like setting the rhythm of your day. Just as you wouldn't leave the house without brushing your teeth or combing your hair, setting aside time each day for devotions anchors your day with purpose and intention. But how do you fit it into a busy schedule filled with school, activities, and time with friends and family?

Start by prioritizing devotionals, just like anything else important in your life. Early mornings work best when the world is quiet, and you're fresh from a good night's sleep. Evenings are better for unwinding and reflecting on your day. The key is consistency in setting a routine.

Choose a time that works for you and stick to it, making an appointment with God just as you commit to your favorite sport or TV show. **A regular time set aside for God becomes a sacred rhythm in your life,** helping you grow in faith and stay connected to Him amidst the busyness of life. Why not give it a try this week? See how a small change can create a big impact on your day!

Create a Sacred Space

Just as you have a favorite spot for doing homework or reading, creating a special place for devotions can turn this time into something to look forward to. You don't need an elaborate space; it could be a cozy corner of your room with a comfortable chair, a small table, or a nook in your family living area that feels peaceful and private.

The key is to choose a place free from distractions—away from the TV, your phone, or other interruptions. You might add a few items that help you focus, like a scented candle, a beautiful journal, or a small cross or icon. This space becomes your retreat, a physical reminder to step away from the world and into God's presence, where you can pour out your heart and listen to what He says. What would your perfect devotional space look like? Take some time to think about how you could create a particular spot just for you and God.

Choose Devotional Materials

Your goal during devotion time is always to deepen your understanding and connection with God. To start, a good devotional book for tweens can guide you with daily readings and reflections that relate directly to your life and challenges. These books often include stories or thoughts for the day and questions that prompt you to think about your life and faith. Choosing a contemporary translation of the Bible that's easy to understand can make a big difference in how you connect with Scripture.

You might also explore apps and websites designed specifically for young Christians, offering daily devotional readings and Bible studies that are both engaging and interactive. These resources often use videos, images, or games to help you learn and apply biblical truths in a fun and meaningful way. Why not try one of these tools this week and see how it enables you to connect with God in a new way?

Reflective Practices

Adding reflection to your devotional time enhances understanding and helps you apply what you learn to daily life. **Journaling is one great way to do this**. Writing down your thoughts, prayers, and new things you've learned can help clarify your feelings and questions, enhancing your spiritual journey. You can look back over time to see how much you've grown, which can be incredibly encouraging.

Another reflective practice is **drawing or doodling,** which can also be a form of prayer and meditation. As you draw, think about the day's devotional reading, letting the creative process help you connect more deeply with God's word. Reflection turns your devotional time into an engaging part of your faith journey, where you connect with God in a way that moves your heart and spirit.

Establishing daily devotional time is like planting a garden. It would help if you had patience, persistence, and care, but the growth over time is beautiful and fulfilling, bringing color and life to your daily experiences. When you prioritize God, it helps you grow in wisdom, strength, and peace, no matter what comes your way. Why not try journaling or drawing this week and see how it adds to your devotional time?

5.2 Worship Beyond Music: Exploring Different Forms of Praise

When you think of worship, what pops into your mind? Perhaps it's singing in the church choir or listening to your favorite worship songs on your playlist. Worship goes beyond melodies and lyrics; it's about expressing your love and reverence for God in many meaningful ways.

The vibrant world of worship goes beyond music. For example, art can be a prayer, like a painter creating beauty with colors on canvas to honor God. Writing poems, stories, or prayers is another fulfilling way to pour out your heart to God in a profoundly personal way. These written expressions of thankfulness, petitions for guidance, or reflections on His word become sacred dialogues between you and God, honoring Him and strengthening your faith. It's about your connection with God, and there's no right or wrong way to do it.

"Express the act of worship in different ways"

Dance is another beautiful way to express worship, as it has been throughout biblical times. Remember how David danced with all his might before the Lord? Like him, dance can celebrate God's presence and express joy and gratitude. It's a meaningful way to connect with God through a physical expression of love and appreciation.

What are some creative ways you might worship God this week? Whether through art, writing, dance, or another form of expression, find what speaks to your heart and brings you closer to Him. Discovering new forms of worship can be as exciting as finding a new favorite hobby. So, why explore and see what resonates with you?

Incorporate Nature in Worship

Imagine stepping outside where the sky is a vast canvas painted with the hues of sunrise or sunset, trees swaying in rhythm to an unseen melody, and air filled with fresh floral scents—all part of God's creation, an open invitation to worship.

Spending time in nature is a profound way to connect with God. Walking through a park, hiking trails, or sitting under a tall tree, take time to see, hear, and smell the wonders around you. Each element of nature, from the smallest leaf to the stars in the sky, reflects God's artistry and love. As you appreciate the natural world around you, it's natural to worship—to thank Him for the beauty surrounding you and to reflect on His power and creativity. This form of worship offers a refreshing change and an opportunity to gain new perspectives and deepen your appreciation for God's artistry in the world.

Why not take a moment this week to explore God's creation? Find a quiet spot outside, take a deep breath, and let the beauty of nature draw you closer to Him. What do you notice that reflects His love and creativity?

Community Worship

While personal acts of worship are vital, joining others in prayer holds unique beauty and strength. **Participating in church services, youth groups, or community prayer meetings** allows you to share in the collective energy and faith of others. Lifting your voices together in prayer and song fosters unity and support within your faith community.

The communal aspect of worship strengthens individual faith and binds the community together in a network of support and encouragement. The collective joy and conviction in such gatherings uplift and remind you that you're part of a larger family of believers walking together in faith.

You develop a more prosperous, more vibrant relationship with God through various expressions of worship—**writing, dancing, embracing nature, and participating in community activities.** Each act of worship is a testament to your faith and a celebration of God's endless love and grace. As you explore diverse forms of prayer, let each moment deepen your reverence and love for God, enriching both your spiritual life and every part of your daily life.

What are some ways you can join with others in worship this week? Whether attending a church service, participating in a youth group, or simply praying with a friend, find an opportunity to connect with your faith community and experience the power of worshiping together.

5.3 Serving Others: Finding Joy in Helping and Giving

Have you ever helped someone and felt a warm glow, almost like you received a gift instead of giving one? That's the joy of serving—like planting seeds of kindness and watching them grow into something beautiful. Serving others is a vital part of living out your faith.

"You can help your friends by making them happy"

Jesus taught through His example and words that serving is not just about doing good deeds; **it's about sharing God's love.** In Matthew 25:35-40, Jesus says that when we feed the hungry, welcome the stranger, or comfort the distressed, it's like doing those things for Him. This Scripture beautifully captures why serving others is so central to the Christian faith—it's a direct way to live Jesus' teachings and show His love to the world.

Identifying where to serve might seem challenging initially, but opportunities are all around you, often closer than you think. Start with your family; maybe a sibling needs help with homework, or a grandparent might appreciate help with chores. In school, look for classmates who might be struggling or lonely—sitting with them at lunch can be an act of service. Your church or local community likely has organized activities like food drives, clothing collections, or visitation programs for the elderly.

These organized efforts make it easy to get involved, providing a structure that makes serving a fun social activity you can enjoy regularly.

The benefits of serving reach far beyond the immediate help you provide. For you, the server, it cultivates a sense of empathy and compassion. When you step into someone else's shoes, even for a moment, you begin to understand their struggles and joys, expanding your perspective and empathy. Such an emotional connection can be profoundly satisfying by connecting you to the whole human family, reminding you that we are all connected and that your actions truly matter.

Serving others spiritually can be a pathway to personal growth. It challenges you to live your beliefs and trust God's guidance as you step out to help others. Each act of service, no matter how small, is a step in your spiritual journey, helping you grow in faith and love.

Let's look at inspiring examples of young people significantly impacted by service. In the Bible, the young boy who offered his loaves and fishes is a great example. With just a small lunch, he played a part in one of Jesus' most famous miracles—feeding 5,000 people. This story shows that no act of service, no matter how small, is insignificant in God's eyes. In more recent times, think about young volunteers who spend their summers building homes for those in need or those who tutor underprivileged children. These young people are not just filling their time; **they're also filling their hearts and others' lives with hope and joy.**

Exploring these opportunities to serve allows you to experience firsthand the joy of giving and the satisfaction of contributing to a cause larger than yourself. It teaches you **compassion, kindness, and the profound impact of simple acts of service.** As you give your time and talents to help others, you meet their physical needs and nurture your spiritual growth and a tangible expression of God's love.

What are some ways you can serve others this week? Whether helping a family member, supporting a friend, or volunteering in your community, find an opportunity to share God's love through your actions.

5.4 The Role of the Church: Connecting with a Faith Community

Imagine walking into a room where everyone is different, yet everyone belongs. Being part of a church community means being yourself, sharing your joys and struggles, and finding guidance and support on your faith journey. The church is a vibrant community of believers who unite to support one another and grow in faith. The church provides:

- Spiritual guidance.
- A sense of belonging.
- Opportunities to serve and be served play a crucial role in life.

The church is a spiritual home where you can deeply connect with God. Through teachings and sermons, you learn about God's word, which guides your understanding and daily application of the Bible. You also engage with your church community through activities like outreach programs and youth groups, where you meet others navigating their faith journeys.

Youth groups provide a range of activities, from Bible study sessions to fun outings, designed to strengthen your faith and help you forge deep friendships. Being part of a choir or worship team allows you to express your faith through music, which can be a profoundly uplifting experience. Volunteer activities contribute to the church's mission and enhance your sense of involvement and belonging.

Being part of a church community means **experiencing joy and strength in fellowship.** Just as the early Christians in the Book of Acts shared their lives, modern church communities offer a support network where members care for each other in times of need and celebrate together in times of joy.

Fellowship is especially crucial during challenging times, as it embodies tangible love and support in Christ. You're never alone as part of a family that grows together in faith and love. In group meetings, church picnics, or prayer groups, each gathering strengthens the bonds between members, creating a resilient web of support that enriches everyone.

Another beautiful aspect of being involved in a church community is appreciating its **diversity.** Churches bring together people from various backgrounds, cultures, and experiences, significantly enriching your faith journey. Diversity shows how different people express their faith and understand God's word, offering opportunities for learning and growth you might not otherwise encounter. For example, listening to testimonies from believers provides insights into the workings of God, where their stories inspire and challenge you to think about your faith in new ways, deepening your understanding and empathy.

When you engage with your church community, you actively participate in a living body of believers journeying together in faith. **You open your heart and spirit to connect, learn, and contribute**, seek opportunities to serve and be served, and lead and be led, ensuring every member feels valued and loved.

Participating in your church community is enriching, offering a foundation of spiritual guidance, communal support, and personal growth. Think of your church as a family reunion, where every face is part of your extended family in Christ, each bringing something unique to the table and creating a richer tapestry of faith and community.

Have you found ways to get involved in your church community? Whether joining a youth group, helping with a church event, or attending services regularly, each step enables you to grow in faith and connect with others on their spiritual journeys.

5.5 Memorizing Scripture: Techniques and Tips to Keep God's Word in Your Heart

Imagine having a treasure chest in your heart, filled with nuggets of wisdom, comfort, and guidance you can access whenever you need them. That's what memorizing Scripture is like—storing **God's precious words** in your heart, always ready to help you, whether you're facing a tough test, a difficult decision, or need encouragement. The words of the Bible are powerful; they can transform your mind, strengthen your faith, and offer comfort during tough times.

"Memorize the word of GOD and keep it in your heart"

Psalm 119:11 says, **"I have hidden your word in my heart that I might not sin against you."** This verse highlights the protective, guiding power of knowing Scripture by heart. By memorizing verses, you arm yourself with God's truth, which guides your decisions and calms your fears, constantly reminding you of His love and promises.

Starting a scripture memorization routine might seem like a big task, but with the proper techniques, it can be a fun and fulfilling part of daily life. One effective method is repetition. **Repeat a verse aloud each morning** as you get ready for school, or write it several times in your journal. This practice reinforces the words in your brain, making it easier to remember them later.

Another helpful technique is visualization. Try to create a mental picture of what a verse means. For example, if you're memorizing Psalm 23—***"The Lord is my shepherd; I shall not want. He makes me lie down in green pastures. He leads me beside still waters"***—imagine those green pastures and still waters, bringing the words to life in your mind. Associating words with images makes memorization fun and deepens your understanding of the verses.

You can easily fit scripture memorization into your daily routines by linking it to things you already do. While brushing your teeth or packing your school bag in the morning, recite a verse you're memorizing. Reflect on that verse at bedtime and consider how it might have applied to your day. Doing so aids in memorization and allows you to start and end your day with God's word. Set a reminder on your phone or computer to review a verse during a break, giving you a little spiritual boost throughout your busy day.

Memorizing Scripture doesn't have to be something you do alone. Why not make it a group activity with friends or family? You could start a small group with friends and challenge each other to memorize a verse each week. Meeting up to recite the verses and discuss what they mean can make the experience more engaging and help you understand the scriptures more deeply. This shared practice strengthens friendships and brings you closer to God.

Scripture memorization is more than just a way to keep your mind sharp; it's a spiritual habit that enriches your faith, prepares you for life's challenges, and deepens your relationship with God. As you fill your heart with God's word, you'll see its transformative power in your life, shaping your thoughts, actions, and reactions daily.

Have you ever tried memorizing a verse? What's one verse you'd like to learn this week?

Here Are Some Verse Ideas to Inspire You! Scan the QR code.

5.6 Faith as a Shield: Protecting Yourself with God's Truth

Imagine stepping into a day armed with more than just your backpack and smartphone—instead, having a shield (not the heavy metal kind knights used), but a shield made of faith, light, and strength. The idea comes from Ephesians 6:10-18, where Paul explained putting on the whole armor of God to stand against life's challenges and temptations. Among these pieces of spiritual armor, he mentions the Shield of Faith to "extinguish all the flaming arrows of the evil one." This metaphor highlights how faith can protect and sustain you, especially during tough times when doubts and fears are like arrows aimed to weaken your spirit.

The Shield of Faith isn't just for epic battles; it has practical applications in your everyday life. When peer pressure tries to sway you to make choices that don't align with your values, **faith can be your shield, providing strength to say no to a path that doesn't feel right for you.** Or think about times when you had to make difficult decisions, about standing up for a friend or choosing honesty over convenience. In those moments, faith provides the wisdom and courage to make decisions that honor God and reflect who you are. Each time you choose faith over fear or peer pressure, you strengthen your shield, making it more robust and reliable.

Challenges and trials are complex, but also **opportunities to fortify your faith**. Just as exercising strengthens muscles, facing tests reinforces your faith. Every challenge you face is an opportunity to trust God and lean on His word. For example, when you're worried about a big exam or a sports tryout, those are perfect times to practice faith by praying for peace and strength. When you see God's faithfulness bringing you through these trials, your trust in Him grows, and your shield becomes more powerful. Remember, this is not about shielding yourself from every problem but facing them with God by your side, knowing you're not alone.

Keeping your shield strong is staying connected to God's word. **The Bible is filled with truths about God and how much He loves you**—truths that dispel fears and doubts. Making a habit of reading the Bible daily and praying keeps these truths fresh to reinforce faith. These practices are like maintenance for your shield, ensuring its readiness and resilience. The peace and confidence that come from knowing God's truth protects you and can change how you face each day, turning challenges into opportunities to see God's power at work. As you grow in faith and learn more about God's truth, remember the power of your Shield of Faith, an excellent tool for defending against challenges and living confidently and purposefully daily.

"Reading the word of God and praying will make you have the armor of God"

As we wrap up this chapter on growing in faith, consider how you've seen faith work. Each prayer, moment of trust, and choice with God builds your shield and deepens your connection. You're ready now to step into the next chapter of your life. Keep your Shield of Faith polished and prepared, knowing that you are ready for anything with God.

ACTIVITY - CHAPTER 5

Scan the QR code to start the activity.

Chapter 6

Exploring Core Christian Values

Imagine this: Every word you say and every action you take is like tossing a pebble into a calm pond. That pebble makes ripples that spread out far beyond where it landed. In the same way, the values we believe in—like being truthful, kind, patient, thankful, brave, and humble—create ripples of joy, fulfillment, and inspiration in our lives and the lives of those around us.

In this chapter, we'll explore what it means to live by these core Christian values. Think of them as a map that helps you navigate the ups and downs of growing up. Let's start with honesty, one of the most essential building blocks of a good life. Living by these values not only creates positive ripples in our lives and the lives of those around us, but also empowers us with personal growth, confidence, and a sense of purpose.

6.1 Honesty: Living Truthfully in a Deceptive World

Honesty is like the North Star—a bright guide in the night sky that helps us find our way. In the Bible, honesty isn't just a suggestion; it's an explicit instruction from God. Proverbs 12:22 says, **"The Lord detests lying lips, but he delights in trustworthy people."** This verse reminds us that being truthful makes God happy because it reflects His character.

But what does it mean to live honestly? It means being real in everything you do—telling the truth when a friend asks for your opinion or admitting when you've made a mistake. Honesty builds trust, the foundation of solid and healthy friendships and relationships. Without honesty, relationships can break apart because of lies and mistrust.

Dishonesty can have significant consequences. If you're not truthful, it can lead to guilt and stress, especially since one lie often leads to another. In your friendships, being dishonest can make others doubt you. For example, if you cheat on a test and your friends find out, they might worry that you could lie too. Trust is fragile and can take a long time to rebuild once it's broken.

The Bible consists of stories about people who chose to be honest, even when it was tough.

Think about Daniel—he lived in Babylon, far from home, and refused to lie or break God's rules. Even when risky, he stayed honest and trustworthy, which led to him finding favor with God and the people around him. Daniel's story shows us that honesty can lead to unexpected blessings.

Want to practice being more honest? Try setting small honesty challenges for yourself. For example, commit to a week without telling any "white lies," even if they seem harmless. Or practice giving honest feedback to a friend or family member when they ask for your opinion, but do it kindly. These little challenges help make honesty a habit.

Remember, being truthful isn't always the easiest choice. It takes courage to be honest, especially when telling the truth might get you into trouble. But the peace and trust that come from being honest are worth much more than any short-term gain from lying. As you practice honesty, you become more like Jesus, who is **"the way, the truth, and the life."** You shine brightly through your commitment to truth as someone others can trust in a world where dishonesty is often easier.

6.2 Kindness: Small Acts with Big Impact

Kindness is like a gentle wave reaching far beyond its first touch. A simple smile or a kind word can create a ripple effect, brightening someone's day or warming their heart long after it happens. The story of the Good Samaritan from the Bible beautifully shows this idea. In this story, a man was hurt and left by the roadside, and while many people walked past him, one man—a Samaritan—stopped to help. He went out of his way to ensure the man was cared for, showing love without any boundaries or prejudice. This transformative power of kindness gives us hope and optimism for a better world.

Now, imagine if kindness was part of your everyday life. You could make kindness a habit, something you do without even thinking. It could be as simple as greeting your teachers and classmates with a smile each day, offering to help someone without waiting to be asked, or choosing words that lift people instead of bringing them down. When kindness becomes part of who you are, it can change your life and encourage others to spread kindness.

Here are some fun and easy ways to show kindness in your community:

1. **Write a thank-you note**: Take a few minutes to write a note to someone who made your day better. It could be a teacher, a friend, or a family member. Let them know how much you appreciate them!

2. **Help a neighbor**: Look for simple ways to help out in your neighborhood. You could walk a neighbor's dog, help carry groceries or rake leaves.

3. **Volunteer your time**: Find a local group or organization that could use your help, like a food bank, community garden, or animal shelter.

4. **Make friendship bracelets**: Create simple bracelets and give them to your classmates or donate them to a local hospital to cheer up other kids.

5. **Start a free library**: Set up a little book exchange box in your neighborhood where people can take and leave a book. It's a great way to share stories and spread kindness!

The best part? Acts of kindness make you feel good, too! You could even start a kindness journal where you write down all the kind things you do or see others do. Note how people react—did someone smile in surprise or even tear up a little? How did those reactions make you feel? Over time, your journal will become a special reminder of how mighty kindness can be and how it brightens the world. Even minor acts can leave a big impression on someone's heart.

By practicing kindness every day and reflecting on it, you'll see how it improves the lives of others and fills your own life with joy, purpose, and connection. Remember, every kind act, no matter how small, helps make the world a brighter, more beautiful place!

6.3 Patience and Understanding God's Timing

Patience is like waiting for a butterfly to come out of its cocoon. You can't rush it; it happens when the time is right. Galatians 5:22-23 in the Bible highlights patience as an essential quality, listing it alongside love, joy, peace, and other virtues from living by the Spirit. Patience means keeping a good attitude and trusting God's timing, even when things aren't happening as quickly as you'd like. It's about **believing God knows what's best**, even when you wish things would change immediately.

One of the Bible's most powerful stories about patience is the story of **Abraham**. God promised Abraham a son who would lead a great nation, as countless as the stars in the sky. But years went by—decades, even—and there was no son. Abraham could have easily lost hope, but he kept believing in God's promise, even when it seemed impossible. He ultimately received his reward for his patience and faith when his son Isaac was born.

Abraham's story teaches us that patience is often a key part of seeing God's plans come true, even when those plans are different from what we expect. It reminds us that when we're waiting for something—like an answer to a prayer or a change in a tough situation—patience helps keep our faith strong.

"If you can wait on the Lord with patience, you will be rewarded greatly by God"

Learning to be patient can seem complicated, especially when you're excited for something to happen. But there are simple ways to practice patience daily, like mindfulness and prayer.

Mindfulness helps you focus on the present instead of worrying about the future or regretting the past. A simple way to practice mindfulness is to focus on your breathing. When you start to feel impatient or stressed, pause and take ten deep breaths, focusing on the sensation of the air moving in and out of your lungs. This practice helps calm your mind and reminds you that God is always with you, right here and now.

Prayer is another excellent way to grow in patience. Through prayer, you can express your feelings to God—sharing your frustrations, hopes, and desires—while also learning to say, **"Not my will, but Yours be done."** Jesus' prayer in the garden of Gethsemane mirrors this, as He demonstrated His trust in God even during the most challenging times. When you pray regularly, you remind yourself that God's timing is perfect, even if it doesn't align with your plans.

In today's world, where everything seems to happen instantly—like social media updates or online shopping—it can feel like waiting isn't unnecessary.

Seeing others achieve things may cause you to feel left out and wonder why God isn't answering your prayers as quickly.

But patience is a powerful act of faith. It teaches you to trust in God's plan for your life, even when you don't immediately see the results. It helps you find joy and growth in the waiting, understanding that sometimes the **journey is just as important as the destination.**

By practicing patience, you start to experience life on God's terms. It helps you develop other good qualities, like peace and kindness because you trust God's timing. Each moment of waiting is a chance to deepen your faith, learn more about God's character, and grow into the person He wants you to be. So, the next time you feel impatient, remember Abraham looking up at the stars, holding onto a promise that seemed impossible. Like a butterfly emerging, God's plans for you will come to life at the right time.

6.4 Gratitude: Cultivating a Thankful Heart Every Day

Imagine each day is like a blank canvas ready for you to paint. Every moment is a different color that fills the canvas to create a picture of your day. Now, think about adding particular strokes of color called gratitude. Each stroke of gratitude brightens the image, making even the ordinary moments shine. That's what gratitude does—it's about being thankful for the big things and noticing the small, everyday blessings we might overlook.

Being grateful has fantastic benefits for both your mind and Spirit. Research shows that gratitude can lift your mood, make you stronger when things are tough, and even improve your health. It's like food for your soul, helping you stay spiritually strong and emotionally balanced. The Bible talks a lot about gratitude, showing us how important it is to thank God for His care and kindness.

"Be grateful"

One powerful example of gratitude from the Bible is the story of **Paul the Apostle**. Even in prison, Paul didn't let sadness or fear take over. Instead, he wrote letters—now part of the New Testament—filled with thanks and praise. He thanked God for His faithfulness and the early Christians for their support. Paul's letters show us that having a thankful heart can help you get through even the most challenging times. His gratitude was a way of recognizing that God was always with him, no matter what.

So, how can you bring more gratitude into your life? One fun and simple way is to start a gratitude journal. Each day, write down a few things you're thankful for. It could be something minor, like a kind word from a friend, a pretty sunset, or a yummy meal. Over time, as you fill up your journal, you'll see just how many things there are to be thankful for, even on tough days. This practice helps you notice all the good things in your life and feel more connected to God's gifts.

Another great way to practice gratitude is to **create family traditions** around thankfulness. For example, you could start a tradition where each family member shares something they are thankful for at dinner. This practice helps bring the family closer together and makes gratitude a regular part of daily life. It reminds everyone that no matter what happens each day, there's always something to be grateful for. These moments of sharing are like building blocks of joy and strength for your family, helping everyone find the good in the everyday hustle and bustle.

Gratitude is especially powerful during tough times. Finding something to be thankful for can completely change how you feel when things are hard. If you're having a rough time with a subject in school, instead of feeling frustrated, try to find something to be grateful for, like having a teacher willing to help you or having the chance to learn new things. This shift in focus enables you to see the good things around you, even when some things aren't going well.

As you practice gratitude daily—through journaling, family traditions, or changing your perspective when things are tough—you'll find that gratitude does more than make you feel better. It deepens your faith and strengthens your relationship with God. You start to see His hand in all the blessings and even in the challenges, knowing that each day is a special gift filled with chances to grow closer to Him. By being grateful, you learn to live with a thankful heart for what you have and hope for what's yet to come. Trust that God is with you every step of the way, helping you paint your life's canvas with colors of grace and love.

6.5 Courage: Be Brave with God on Your Side

What do you think of when you hear the word "courage"? It could be a superhero from your favorite movie or someone facing danger without fear. But in real life, courage is about trusting that God is with you, even when you feel afraid.

A great example of courage from the Bible is the story of **David and Goliath.** In this story, David, a young shepherd boy, faces Goliath, a giant Philistine warrior challenging the Israelites to a fight. Goliath is heavily armed and much more potent than any soldier in Israel's army, causing great fear among them. Despite being just a young shepherd, David wasn't intimidated. He didn't have super strength or a giant warrior's armor. What he did have was faith in God's power. That faith gave him the courage to face Goliath with just a sling and a few stones. David struck Goliath on the forehead with a single stone, defeating him. David trusted God to help him win, teaching us a lesson about courage that we can apply to our daily lives, no matter the challenges we face.

Building courage starts with small steps. Consider your small fears, such as speaking up in class, trying out for a sports team, or standing up for a friend being teased. Pick one slight fear to face each week. Before you face it, take a few moments to pray and ask God to give you strength and confidence.

Find a Bible verse that helps you feel brave when you're scared. A good example is Joshua 1:9, which says, **"Have I not commanded you? Be strong and courageous. Do not be afraid; do not be discouraged, for the Lord your God will be with you wherever you go."** This verse is a powerful reminder that God is always with you. Every small act of bravery builds up your courage a little more, making more considerable challenges seem less scary.

Consider ways to step out of your comfort zone to grow your faith. Maybe you could share your story about how you came to believe in God with a friend or volunteer for a leadership role in your church youth group. Doing brave things helps you grow spiritually and shows others how to trust God. Every time you act courageously, you show others what it means to follow God.

To bring this idea to life, look at some modern examples of courage shown by young people like you.

Think about Malala Yousafzai, a young girl from Pakistan who stood up for her right to go to school, even when it was dangerous. Her courage sparked a global movement for girls' education. Then there's **Greta Thunberg**, a teen from Sweden who started an international movement to fight climate change. She spoke bravely to world leaders and demanded action, even when people criticized her. These stories demonstrate that age does not limit courage. They remind us that we can make a difference in the world by using our faith and the courage to stand up for what we believe in.

Each courageous step is toward becoming the person God wants you to be. Remember, courage doesn't mean you're not afraid; it means you face your fears with faith. Every brave act shows your trust in God's strength and helps you believe that you can face anything with God by your side. So, when you see challenges or opportunities ahead, hold on to your faith, step out with courage, and watch how God works through you to do amazing things.

6.6 Humility: The Beauty of Putting Others First

Imagine walking into a room where everyone is trying to talk over each other, each person trying to prove they're the most interesting, the smartest, or successful. Now, picture a different room where people listen closely to each other, appreciate each other's ideas, and celebrate each other's successes. The second room creates a much more welcoming and cheerful atmosphere. This is what humility looks like, allowing each person the chance to shine and fostering a space where everyone can learn and grow. Humility is often mistaken for putting yourself down or lacking confidence, but it's about recognizing your worth and appreciating the cost of others. Everyone has something unique to contribute.

Jesus is the best example of humility. As shown in the Bible, Jesus demonstrated true humility throughout His life. Philippians 2:3- 8 tells us that even though Jesus was God, He didn't hold onto that status. Instead, Jesus humbled Himself by becoming a servant. He even washed His disciples' feet, a job usually done by the lowest servant. He spent time with people whom society ignored or looked down on. Everything Jesus did was filled with humility and love, showing us that true greatness isn't about being the best or most essential but helping others feel important.

How can you practice humility in your life? Start by listening more than you speak. When you're conversing, give the other person your full attention. Ask questions about what they think or feel. It would help to share your stories, but ensure you're not always the first to talk.

Another way to show humility is by recognizing the efforts of others. Whether working on a school project, playing on a sports team, or helping out at home, make it a habit to notice and praise the efforts of those around you. This acknowledgment helps others feel valued and reminds you that success is often the result of teamwork.

"You celebrating your friends shows you're humble"

Serving others without seeking praise is another excellent way to practice humility. Look for chances to help out quietly without expecting to be noticed. You can set up chairs before a school event, help clean up after a class, or assist a classmate struggling with homework. Doing these acts of service without looking for attention can be rewarding and is a true sign of humble service.

Humility can transform your relationships and create a ripple effect of kindness around you. In friendships, humility means celebrating your friends' successes just as if they were your own, which strengthens your bonds. In your family, humility helps you see and appreciate all the little things everyone does to support each other. Even in difficult situations, approaching problems can lead to better solutions that respect everyone's feelings and create a path for accurate understanding.

Remember, being humble doesn't mean thinking less of yourself; it means thinking about yourself less and focusing more on how you can support and uplift those around you. By embracing humility, you follow Jesus' example and help create an environment where everyone can grow and succeed together. This approach to life deepens your connection with others and with God, as you learn to see and appreciate the value in everyone, including yourself.

In this chapter on exploring core Christian values, we've seen how honesty, kindness, patience, gratitude, courage, and humility can significantly impact your life and the world around you. Each value is like a thread in the fabric of a well-lived life, reflecting the love and truth found in the Gospel. Next, we'll discover how living out these values can shape your character and future, guiding you to live a meaningful life with a faith that shines brightly in a hopeful world.

ACTIVITY - CHAPTER 6

Scan the QR code to start the activity.

Chapter 7

Embracing Personal Growth

Imagine you're the captain of a ship sailing across a vast ocean, heading toward a treasure island. Just like a captain needs a map and a compass to find the hidden treasure, you need your tools and plan to navigate the exciting journey of personal growth. This chapter is your map, guiding you on how to grow closer to God and become the best version of yourself. It's all about setting goals, learning from each experience, and keeping track of your progress, just like a captain marks each vital milestone on their voyage.

7.1 Setting Goals with God: Planning Your Spiritual Growth

Have you ever thought about setting goals for your spiritual life? For example, you might set goals for school, such as getting better grades or making new friends, but setting spiritual goals can help you focus on growing your faith. These goals aren't just ordinary; they're **SMART**: Specific, Measurable, Achievable, Relevant, and Time-bound. This means each goal is clear and well-defined, includes a method to track progress, is realistic and essential for your spiritual growth, and has a set deadline to keep you motivated.

The Concept of Spiritual Goals

Think about the areas of your spiritual life where you want to grow. Maybe you want to understand the Bible better, improve how often and deeply you pray or show more love through acts of kindness and service. These are just starting points. For example, a specific goal could be to read the Bible for 15 minutes every morning before school to understand God's word better, making it clear and time-bound. Or, you could set a goal to volunteer at the local community center once a month to practice serving others, which is achievable and relevant to living out your faith.

Guide to Setting Spiritual Goals

Start with prayer when setting your goals. Ask God to show you the areas where He wants you to grow. Reflect on passages like Micah 6:8, which reminds you of what God desires from you—to act justly, love mercy, and walk humbly with Him. This reflection can help you identify which parts of your spiritual life need more attention. Next, write down your goals using the SMART framework. Ensure each goal is specific and clear, with a plan to track your progress. For example, if your goal is to improve your prayer life, you might keep a prayer journal to record your prayers and God's answers.

"Set goals how you will build your spiritual life"

Prayer and Goal Setting

Remember, prayer isn't just about asking for things; it's a conversation with God. When setting your goals, keep that conversation going. Ask God for guidance on which goals to set and the strength to achieve them. Include a prayer log as part of your goal tracker, noting when you pray about your goals and how God is responding. This practice turns your goal-setting into a spiritual journey, deepening your connection with God.

Create a Goal Tracker

A goal tracker can be anything from a simple notebook to a section in your planner or even a digital app designed for tracking progress. It's a place where you write down each goal and the steps to achieve it. You can also note milestones, like finishing a book of the Bible or getting involved in a new ministry at church. To make tracking more fun and motivating, consider using visual elements like stickers or colored pens to mark your progress. Some digital apps even offer reminders and motivational quotes to help keep you focused and inspired.

A structured approach to growing your faith brings clarity and purpose to your spiritual journey. It turns vague desires for growth into specific, trackable actions, making your spiritual growth intentional and visible, just like a ship captain marks their journey on a map, steadily moving closer to the treasure.

7.2 Learning from Mistakes: What Failure Teaches

Think about the last time you tripped over something in your path. Did you stop walking completely, look to see what caused you to stumble, step over it, and keep going? Just like a physical stumble, mistakes in life are unavoidable, but they don't have to halt your progress. Instead, they can serve as valuable lessons that help you navigate your path more wisely. Everyone makes mistakes—your friends, family, and even leaders in the Bible. These slip-ups are a natural part of learning and growing, especially in your spiritual journey.

"Think of your mistakes and learn from them"

Normalize the Experience of Failure

Mistakes can sometimes make you feel like you're falling behind or failing at being good, but remember that everyone you admire has made mistakes and learned from them. In the Bible, Peter, one of Jesus' closest followers, made a big mistake when he denied knowing Jesus during a critical moment. Despite this, Peter went through a journey of learning and growth that transformed him into one of the most influential leaders in the early church. His story shows that mistakes, even big ones, are a natural part of growth—not just spiritually but personally and emotionally as well.

Encourage a Growth Mindset

The concept of a growth mindset, introduced by psychologist Carol Dweck, is critical to handling challenges and mistakes. Unlike a fixed mindset, which believes that your character, intelligence, and creative abilities are set and unchangeable, a growth mindset thrives on challenges. It sees failure not as proof of a lack of intelligence or worth but as a positive opportunity for growth and a chance to expand your abilities. When you make a mistake, instead of thinking, "I can't do this," remind yourself that you're learning how to do it. Each mistake is a step in the learning process toward becoming better, stronger, and wiser.

Steps to Recover from Mistakes

When you realize you've made a mistake, the first step is to acknowledge it openly. It doesn't mean being hard on yourself; it means understanding that you're human and, like everyone else, capable of making mistakes. After acknowledging the error, seek forgiveness if it has hurt someone. It could be from God, a friend, or a family member. Seeking forgiveness is a humbling process that helps repair relationships and brings peace to your heart. Next, take some time to reflect on what led to the mistake. Was it a lack of knowledge, fear, poor planning, or something else?

Understanding the cause of the mistake helps you avoid making the same error in the future. Finally, plan for similar situations differently moving forward. It might involve setting reminders, asking for advice, practicing a skill, or praying for strength and wisdom.

Reflective Journaling Prompt: Keeping a Mistake Journal

To help you learn from your mistakes:

1. Try starting a mistake journal.
2. Please write it down in your journal whenever you make a big or small mistake.
3. Please include details about what happened and why you think it happened.
4. Reflect on what the mistake taught you, and note one or two things you plan to do differently next time.

The purpose of this exercise isn't to dwell on the mistake but to see your growth and learning over time. It can be incredibly empowering to look back at your journal and see how far you've come—how many mistakes you've learned from and how they have contributed to your growth.

By understanding and embracing the lessons that mistakes offer, you'll be better prepared to face life's challenges with resilience and wisdom. Mistakes aren't roadblocks; they're stepping stones that help guide your growth and refine your character. By handling them with grace and a growth mindset, you prepare yourself for future challenges, ready to seize opportunities for personal and spiritual development.

7.3 The Importance of Self-Reflection: Understanding Your Spiritual Journey

Have you considered why looking in a mirror is a standard part of your day? You check in with yourself before you step out into the world. Self-reflection in your spiritual life works similarly to a mirror. It gives you a moment to pause, look inward, and assess how you're growing in your faith and personal development. Self-reflection is a powerful tool that helps you understand who you are, how you're progressing, and where you might need more focus or change.

Teach Methods of Self-Reflection

Self-reflection can take many forms, offering unique insights into your spiritual and personal growth. **Prayer** is one of the most direct ways to reflect; it allows you to speak openly with God about your hopes, struggles, and questions. It's also a time to listen, quiet your mind, and hear what God is speaking into your heart.

Another method is **meditation**, where you focus on a specific thought, scripture, or idea. This practice allows deeper insights to emerge as you ponder and breathe deeply. **Writing in a spiritual diary** is another powerful method. In your diary, you can write prayers, list things you're grateful for, or express your thoughts and feelings about your faith journey. Each entry is a snapshot of where you are at that moment in your spiritual walk.

Encourage Regular Reflection

"Sometimes you have to look at the mirror not to see how beautiful you are but to self reflect"

Making self-reflection a regular part of your life brings many benefits. It helps you see how you're growing, recognize areas where you might struggle, and identify aspects of your character or faith that need nurturing. Regular reflection can also deepen your relationship with God by encouraging open, honest dialogue about your life and faith.

For example, setting aside time each week to review your spiritual diary can provide insights into handling challenges, responding to answered prayers, and growing your understanding of Biblical teachings. Over time, this regular practice will highlight your spiritual growth, showing you where you've been and giving you a sense of where God might lead you next.

Reflective Questions

Reflect on thought-provoking questions to deepen your faith and assess your spiritual health. Ask yourself, "When have I felt closest to God this week? What led me to those moments?" or "When did I find it difficult to live out my faith?" These questions encourage you to think carefully about your daily walk with God and help you recognize specific situations that strengthen or challenge your faith. You might also ask, "How have my prayers been answered recently?" or "What scripture spoke to me this week, and why?" Reflecting on these questions can foster greater self-awareness and strengthen your daily commitment to living out your faith.

Reflective Activities

One engaging activity to visualize your faith journey is drawing a timeline of your spiritual growth. Start by marking significant moments when you felt a shift or growth in your faith—maybe when you made a tough decision with God's guidance, experienced a moment of doubt, felt a mighty prayer, or participated in a service project that changed your perspective. Seeing these moments visually can help you appreciate your progress by recognizing God's presence. This timeline can become a living document you add to as you grow and experience life with God by your side.

Through regular reflection, you create a rich tapestry of self-awareness and spiritual insight, ensuring that your faith remains a vibrant and growing part of your daily life. Remember that each insight and moment of understanding brings you closer to a more fulfilling relationship with God and gives you a clearer view of your spiritual path.

7.4 Growing Through Service: Lessons Learned From Helping Others

When you think of service, you might picture community projects or helping at church, but serving others is really about embodying the love and humility that Jesus demonstrated. Think about Jesus washing His disciples' feet; this wasn't just a simple act but a powerful demonstration of service and humility. Through serving, you grow in your spiritual journey, learning lessons of compassion, empathy, and God's love in action.

Serving others is a unique way to grow spiritually because it puts your faith into action, helping you understand and live out Jesus' teachings more deeply. For example, when you help someone in need, you are following the commandment to love your neighbor as yourself. This hands-on application of Jesus' teachings can deepen your faith and give you a better understanding of what it means to be a follower of Christ. You're putting theory into practice, making the principles of Christianity real and tangible—not just ideas you hear about in Sunday school.

Share Service Project Ideas

"You can also engage yourself in community service to keep an environment"

You might wonder how to get involved in service, especially as a tween. There are plenty of age-appropriate service projects that you can participate in to make a big difference. For example, you could organize a book drive for children who don't have access to a library. You might gather some friends to help clean up a local park or spend an afternoon visiting a nearby nursing home, playing games with the residents, or reading to them. At school, you could tutor classmates who are struggling in subjects you excel in.

You can help set up events at church or join the choir. Each of these activities helps others and allows you to see the impact of your actions, encouraging your spiritual growth and expanding your understanding of how to serve God by serving others.

Reflect on Service Experiences

After participating in service projects, take time to reflect on your experiences. How did helping others make you feel? Did you learn anything new about yourself, the people you helped, or your faith? Reflection can be enlightening through journaling or discussing your experiences with friends, family, or youth groups. You might write about helping a neighbor or how you felt God's presence while serving others. This reflection helps solidify what you've learned and experienced, deepens your gratitude for the opportunity to assist others, and highlights its impact on your faith journey.

Testimonies of Growth Through Service

Hearing stories about others who have found joy and spiritual growth through service can be deeply inspiring.

Consider the story of a fellow tween who organized a community garden to provide fresh produce for needy families. She shared how the project helped the community and taught her about the power of working together and God's endless provision.

Another example is a young boy who volunteered at an animal shelter, which helped him overcome shyness and grow in confidence as he realized that God used him to make a difference in the lives of others. These stories highlight the transformative power of service—it helps those in need and brings blessings to those who serve, showing how acts of kindness can ripple outward, changing lives and hearts.

By engaging in service, reflecting on your experiences, and listening to the stories of others, you gain a deeper understanding of yourself, your community, and your faith. It's a way to live out the teachings of Jesus, who came to serve. Through service, you discover that true joy and growth come from looking outward and caring for others. As you continue to serve and grow, remember that each act of service is a step toward becoming more like Jesus, shaping you with compassion, faith, and deep love.

7.5 Your Role in God's Story: Where You Fit in the Big Picture

Imagine a grand tapestry where each thread, color, and pattern plays a vital role in creating a beautiful masterpiece.

This tapestry is like God's story—a vast, ongoing narrative of creation, fall, redemption, and restoration stretching from the beginning of time into eternity. Everyone, including you, has a unique role in this story, carefully woven by God's hand. Understanding this story helps you see and find your place within the bigger picture.

God's Overarching Story

The story begins with creation, where God made everything in the world, declaring it all very good. Humans were created to live in harmony with God, each other, and all of creation. But then the fall occurred; sin entered the world through Adam and Eve's disobedience, distorting everything and separating humanity from God. However, the story doesn't end there. God set a plan for redemption, culminating in Jesus's life, death, and resurrection, offering salvation to all.

Today, we live in the age of the church, where we, as followers of Christ, are called to spread the good news and serve as agents of God's love. We will continue to do this until restoration, when God renews heaven and earth and dwells with us in perfect unity.

Identify Personal Roles

Think about how you fit into this incredible narrative. Your talents, interests, and experiences aren't random; they're gifts and callings that equip you to play your part in God's story. For example, if you have a talent for communication, perhaps your role involves sharing God's love through storytelling or teaching. If you love art, you might be meant to create works that reflect God's glory and draw others to Him.

Your experiences, including your challenges, help you connect with others going through similar trials, offering them the same hope and comfort you've found in God.

Active Participation

You can find active participation in God's purpose in everyday acts of faithfulness. It can include sharing the good news of Jesus with a friend, serving those in need in your community, or using your creative talents—like art, music, or writing—to glorify God and inspire others. Each action plays a part in unfolding God's story. Think of small ways to start. Maybe you could join a Bible study group, volunteer at a local charity, or start a prayer journal where you write down prayers for your friends and family. Each step you take is an act of participation in God's redemptive work.

Inspiring Stories of Purposeful Living

Consider the inspiring story of Lily, who discovered her passion for music and used her talent to lead worship in her youth group. Through this role, she deepened her faith and touched her peers' hearts, encouraging them in their spiritual journeys.

Then there's Jordan, a teen with a knack for technology, who started a blog to share his struggles and triumphs in faith. He created a digital space where teens could find encouragement and community. Stories like these show how understanding and embracing your role in God's story can lead to a life filled with purpose and impact, helping you fulfill the unique mission God has planned for you.

Viewing your life as part of God's grand narrative gives you a sense of belonging and purpose beyond the everyday. You're participating in a divine story, contributing to a masterpiece that's still being created. As you continue to explore and embrace your role, remember that every small act of faith, every step in your growth, and every use of your talents is an essential thread in the beautiful tapestry of God's unfolding story.

7.6 Leadership and Faith: Be a Godly Influence Among Peers

When you hear the word leader, what images come to mind? Maybe you think of a president, a CEO, or a school principal. However, leadership, especially in a Christian context, is about influencing others positively by embodying qualities like humility, service, and integrity—traits that Jesus demonstrated. Christian leadership means leading by serving, guiding by example, and putting others before yourself. It involves making decisions that align with God's teachings and helping others see the light of God through your actions and choices.

Godly Leadership

"Be a leader who leads with integrity"

In the realm of faith, a leader guides others on a path toward Christ. This type of leadership is marked by humility—recognizing that every ability you have is a gift from God and using those gifts to serve others.

Integrity is another cornerstone, ensuring your actions align with your words, both in public and private. Finally, service involves a commitment to put the needs of others before your own, defining what it means to lead in a godly way. These qualities ensure that your leadership lifts up those around you and points them toward God.

Examples of Young Leaders in the Bible

Timothy and Josiah are fantastic examples of young leaders who made significant impacts. Timothy, a young disciple of Paul, was entrusted with leading one of the early Christian communities. Despite his youth, Timothy was known for his faith and dedication—qualities that Paul encouraged him to rely on rather than his age. Josiah became king of Judah at just eight years old and led a major religious reform in his kingdom, guiding his people back to worship God despite the idolatrous practices that had taken hold. Both figures demonstrate that age does not determine the ability of God; what truly matters are God's principles, faith, and commitment.

Practical Leadership Skills

Leadership involves practical skills like effective communication—sharing your thoughts clearly and listening to others to achieve understanding. **Decision-making** is another crucial skill, requiring choices that align with their principles, even when unpopular. **Conflict resolution** means handling disagreements with grace and wisdom, ensuring that solutions are fair, and promoting aren't rather than division. These skills are for officially designated leaders; they are tools every Christian can use to positively influence their family, friends, classmates, and community members.

Encourage Leadership Opportunities

Look for opportunities to practice leadership in everyday life. You could volunteer in your youth group to help organize events or lead a small group discussion. At school, you might run for a position in student government or take the lead on a group project. You could also join or start a community service project to address a local need. Each role allows you to practice making decisions, resolving conflicts, and communicating while serving others and modeling Christ-like behavior.

Leadership is about much more than just being in charge. It's about positively impacting those around you by living your faith boldly and authentically. By developing leadership skills and taking on leadership roles, you enhance your ability to guide others and grow spiritually to become more like Jesus, who came to serve others.

As we conclude this chapter on embracing personal growth, remember that each aspect we explored contributes to your development as a committed person of faith. Every step prepares you for the life God calls you to live. As you grow in your understanding and practice of these principles, you'll find yourself stronger in your faith and more equipped to influence the world around you in positive, life-changing ways.

The next chapter focuses on preparing for the future, guiding you to set long-term goals, face new challenges, and grow your character. This next step will help you apply what you've learned about personal growth to broader aspects of life and faith, preparing you for whatever comes your way.

ACTIVITY - CHAPTER 7

Scan the QR code to start the activity.

Chapter 8

Preparing for the Future

Imagine a beautiful forest filled with winding paths through tall trees, each leading to new and exciting adventures. Like your future, this forest is full of possibilities, choices, and dreams waiting to come true. As you stand ready to explore, remember you're not navigating the forest alone. God is with you, guiding each step, lighting your way, and planting dreams in your heart that can grow into beautiful realities.

8.1 Dreaming Big with God: How to Trust God with Your Dreams

"Trust God with your dreams"

Envision a Future with God

Have you ever considered what your life might look like five, ten, or even twenty years from now? Dreaming about the future is fun and an essential part of growing up. God is deeply interested in your dreams. Jeremiah 29:11 assures you that He has plans to give you hope and a bright future.

When you dream with God, you explore the fantastic possibilities He has in store for you. Picture yourself achieving your biggest goals—maybe as an artist displaying work in a gallery, a scientist making groundbreaking discoveries, or a leader shaping new ideas and paths. God places dreams in your heart that align with the unique talents He has given you, and He takes joy in helping you fulfill them.

Dream Fulfillment from the Bible

The Bible is filled with stories of people for whom God gave great dreams and promises. Think of Joseph, who had specific dreams about his future that seemed impossible then. Imagine a young shepherd boy becoming an influential leader in Egypt. Despite facing many challenges and detours, God's plan for Joseph unfolded precisely as He intended, and Joseph's dreams came true.

Esther, too, was an ordinary Jewish girl who became a queen and saved her people. Her story beautifully reminds us that God places us where He wants us to be and can turn the biggest dreams into reality. These stories show that no matter how big your dreams are when they align with God's plan, He will guide you to make them come true.

Practical Steps to Align Dreams with God's Will

Prayer is not just a way to align your dreams with God's will, it's a powerful tool that empowers you. You can talk to God anytime about your hopes and dreams, sharing everything with Him, big or small. As you pray, ask God to open the doors He wants for you and close the ones that aren't part of His plan. Seek godly counsel from people you trust—like parents, teachers, or pastors—who can offer wisdom and guidance. They can help align your dreams with God's word and His path for you. Most importantly, remember that patience and trusting God's timing are essential. He knows the best time for every season in your life, and His timing is always perfect.

Create a Dream Journal

Starting a dream journal is not just a task, it's the beginning of an exciting journey. Use it to record all your dreams, big and small—a special place for your heart's desires and for discovering God's plan for your life. Whenever you have a new dream, jot it down. Write about the steps you might take to achieve that dream. Keep track of prayers about your dreams and note any answers or signs God gives you. Over time, your journal will become a precious record of your journey with God, filled with dreams realized through His grace.

Remember that God is the ultimate dreamer as you navigate your dreams and plans. He designed the oceans, mountains, and stars in the sky—and dreamed of you, with all your unique talents and potential. Dreaming big with God means embracing His incredible plans for you, as vast as the ocean and as high as the heavens. So, take His hand, step into the forest of your future, and let the adventure begin.

8.2 Transitioning to Teen Years: Keeping God Close When Everything Changes

As you edge closer to your teen years, think of it as entering a new season filled with growth, change, and new experiences. This season will bring about transformations both outside and inside.

Physically, you'll notice changes in your body as you grow. Emotionally, your feelings may become more robust and more complex. Socially, your relationships with friends and family might shift in new ways. It's like receiving a whole new set of tools; some might initially feel unfamiliar.

But remember, every change is an opportunity to grow, and with God by your side, you can navigate every change with confidence and grace.

"Stay connected with God"

One of the most significant parts of entering your teenage years is determining your identity. During this time, you start to figure out who you are and what you want to be—it's like an artist with a blank canvas deciding what to paint.

Faith plays a crucial role, like a palette of colors you use to paint your canvas. With a strong foundation of trust, you can create a vibrant picture of yourself as the person God created you to be. Keeping God close will help you stay rooted in values that bring out the best in you, no matter how much the world changes around you.

Staying connected to God during these transformative years is critical, and there are practical ways to nurture your relationship with Him. Regular worship, personal prayer time, church services, and youth group meetings keep your faith active and alive. These practices act as anchors, keeping you steady amid the changing waters of teenage life. Finding a youth group can provide a supportive community where you can share and grow with peers, explore their faith, offering companionship, encouragement, and insights from their experiences

Mentorship is not just about guidance, it's about finding a companion in your journey. Having a mentor who walks closely with God is like having a guide in unfamiliar territory. A mentor can offer guidance, wisdom, and a listening ear. They can help you navigate difficult decisions, encourage you when you're struggling, and celebrate your successes. To find a mentor, look to your parents, grandparents, church, school, or community leaders who demonstrate the kind of faith and character you admire. Meet your mentor regularly to discuss life, faith, and your future. Mentorship can be a powerful source of support and encouragement as you grow.

As you enter your teenage years, remember that this new season is a beautiful opportunity for growth and discovery. With each change, you can learn more about yourself, deepen your faith, and shape your identity. Keep God at the center during this time, and watch how beautifully He paints your life with His love and purpose.

8.3 Responsibilities: Balancing Life with Grace

As you grow and step into a new chapter of life, you'll find that your responsibilities naturally increase. At first, these responsibilities may feel heavier as you figure out how to balance schoolwork, family time, hanging out with friends, and growing in your faith. Managing it all can sometimes feel overwhelming, but think of it as an opportunity to learn how to balance life with grace and wisdom. Let's explore practical ways to manage your time and responsibilities, keeping stress at bay while reserving space to enjoy life and grow in your faith.

Time Management Skills

Effective time management is like learning a new dance routine. At first, it might seem difficult, and you might miss a step or two, but you'll move more confidently with practice. Start by identifying your daily tasks and responsibilities. You can make a list or use a planner. Prioritize your tasks based on importance. Focus on the tasks that need to be done soon, like homework or an upcoming project, versus those that can wait, like organizing your closet.

Seek God's guidance in setting your priorities. Pray for wisdom to know what needs your attention the most. James 1:5 reminds us that if we lack wisdom, we should ask God, who gives generously to everyone without fault. As you plan, allocate time for tasks, rest, and fun. Create a schedule that includes studying, doing chores, spending time with friends and family, and activities that help you grow spiritually, like Bible study and prayer. Maintaining a proper balance keeps stress at bay and allows you to enjoy life more fully.

Stress Management Through Faith

As your responsibilities increase, stress may sneak in like an uninvited guest. Did you know that faith can be a powerful stress reliever? Turning to prayer, scripture reading, and Christian meditation can be excellent stress management methods. When you feel overwhelmed, take a moment to pause, pray, and hand your worries over to God. Philippians 4:6-7 encourages you not to be anxious but to present your requests to God. In return, He promises to guard your heart and mind with His peace.

Scripture reading can be incredibly soothing. Find verses about peace and God's protection, and memorize a few. These words can be a comforting balm when you're feeling stressed.

Christian meditation involves:

- Spending time in quiet reflection.
- Focusing on God's word.
- Letting His peace fill your mind.

This could mean sitting while reading your Bible, pondering a verse, or listening to worship music and letting its truth settle in your heart.

Learning to Say No

One of the most essential skills you learn as you take on more responsibilities is the **ability to say no.** You might sometimes feel pressured to do everything and please everyone, but it's only occasionally possible or healthy. **Saying no means setting boundaries** and understanding your limits to protect your time and focus on God's calling for you. It isn't selfish; it's wise management of your resources.

When you need to say no, do so kindly but firmly. Explain why you can't take on the task or attend a particular event. Most people will understand. Remember, whenever you say no to something that doesn't align with your life or priorities, you're saying yes to something more substantial. It could mean more time for a project, rest, or activities that help you grow your faith.

Celebrate Small Successes

Amidst the hustle of managing responsibilities, remember to celebrate your successes, no matter how small. Did you finish a difficult assignment or make time for prayer despite a busy day? Celebrate those victories! They're reminders of God's faithfulness and your growth. Recognizing these achievements boosts your morale and motivates you to keep moving forward. You could even keep a success journal to jot down these accomplishments. Looking back on them can be incredibly encouraging, especially when you need to do more.

Managing increased responsibilities means learning to balance your life in a way that honors God, respects your needs, and allows you to thrive. With these strategies, you can handle your responsibilities with efficiency, grace, and peace, knowing that God is helping you manage each day's tasks.

8.4 Preparing for High School: New Challenges and Faith

High school often feels like a giant leap rather than a small step. It's a place filled with new faces, a maze of hallways, and a schedule that can seem like a jigsaw puzzle. You'll encounter more challenging academics and a busier social scene than you're used to. It's like stepping onto a larger stage where everything feels heavier. Amidst these changes, your faith serves as an anchor—a steady, sure presence that helps you navigate high school's exciting, sometimes intimidating environment.

When you think about the challenges of high school, academics come to mind first. The workload is heavier, the material is more challenging, and social dynamics can shift. You'll face tests in your classes and tests of your character and faith.

Friendships might change as everyone learns more about who they are and where they fit in. Peer pressure can intensify, presenting choices that may not always align with your values. Here, faith becomes your compass, guiding you to make decisions that reflect who you are as a follower of Christ and helping you grow into the person God intends you to be.

"Always remember putting smile on your face."

Building a support system in high school means finding friends who share your Christian values and provide spiritual and emotional support. They're like fellow navigators, helping you stay on course when things get tough. You can encourage each other, study the Bible, pray, and share life experiences. Look for youth groups, Christian clubs, or service projects where you can meet other students who share your faith.

Starting a conversation can open the door to a new friendship. Remember, Proverbs 27:17 says, **"As iron sharpens iron, so one person sharpens another."** These friendships can make high school more enjoyable, meaningful, and enriching.

In high school, you'll face numerous decisions, like which clubs to join, how to handle peer pressure, and how to respond to situations that challenge your faith. When you're grounded in your Christian beliefs, these decisions become more accessible to manage because you have a clear sense of right and wrong.

Keep your values close to your heart, and memorize scriptures that address your challenges, such as maintaining purity, honesty, and kindness. When confronted with a difficult choice, ask yourself if it aligns with God's word and what Jesus would want you to do.

Your faith is both a guide and a constant companion to help you manage the pressures of high school life. Make prayer a regular part of your day, especially before school, asking God to guide your steps, words, and actions.

When you feel overwhelmed, turn to Scripture. Verses like Philippians 4:13, **"I can do all this through him who gives me strength,"** remind you of your trustworthy source of strength. Keeping a prayer journal can also be helpful. Write down your concerns, prayers for friends, and the moments you see God working in your life. This practice can help you see how your relationship with God grows and deepens.

As you prepare for high school, remember that you are entering a significant phase of life filled with opportunities for growth, learning, and deepening your faith. With God as your guide, you can face each day with confidence and grace, ready to make the most of your high school years.

8.5 Maintaining Faith in Hard Times: A Guide for Tough Days

Sometimes, life feels like trying to stay balanced in an unexpected storm. Sitting down and waiting for it to pass might seem more manageable. But what if you learned how to dance in the rain instead of waiting out the storm?

Hard times are challenging, but they also offer opportunities to deepen your faith, stay closer to God, and grow into a more robust version of yourself. James 1:2-4 tells us to consider it pure joy whenever we face trials because they test our faith and help us learn perseverance and maturity. Your tough days show what you're made of, so let's discuss ways to keep your faith firm even when things get tough.

Trials can come in many forms—a bad grade, a friend letting you down, or an overwhelming situation at home. In those moments, it might feel like God is far away, but that's when He's closer than ever, ready to listen, comfort, and help you overcome every difficulty. It is where the power of Scripture comes in. Memorizing verses that speak of God's faithfulness and love can be a lifeline during tough times.

For example, Psalm 46:1 reminds us, "**God is our refuge and strength, an ever-present help in trouble**." Or Isaiah 41:10, where God tells us, "**Do not fear, for I am with you**," promising to strengthen and help us. These words aren't just lovely sayings—they're promises from God to you. Write them down, keep them in your heart, and recall them when you feel overwhelmed.

Consider the stories of others who have faced their storms and become stronger. Hearing real-life experiences can be incredibly encouraging. For instance, a teen might share how they dealt with the loss of a grandparent—a time of profound sadness where they found comfort in prayer and their church community. Or perhaps there's a story of someone who felt left out at school but found strength by turning to Bible study and forming new friendships rooted in faith. These testimonies are proof of God's active presence in our lives, showing that no problem is too big or too small for Him to handle.

Prayer is your direct line to God and a powerful tool for building resilience. It's your way to share your fears and invite Him into every situation. But how do you pray in a way that builds resilience? Start by being honest. Tell God exactly how you feel; He can handle your doubts, anger, fear, and questions. Then, ask for what you need—peace, courage, or understanding.

You can use prayers from the Psalms as a guide or create your own. For instance, you might pray, "God, this situation feels bigger than I can handle. Please show me Your strength in my weakness. Help me see this through Your eyes." Remember, resilience doesn't mean you won't ever feel down or scared; it means you know who to turn to when those feelings arise.

Face tough days head-on with God by your side, finding joy not despite challenges but through them, teaching you about God's unending faithfulness. So, the next time you find yourself in a storm, remember these steps and know you have everything you need to endure and thrive. With God, you're growing through your problems, learning to dance in the rain, and equipped with faith, Scripture, testimonies, and strength through prayer.

8.6 Looking Ahead: Continued Growth in Faith and Love

Imagine your faith journey as a garden that you cultivate over time. Like a garden, your spiritual life needs regular care and attention—watering, weeding, and planting new seeds to keep it vibrant and growing. Setting long-term faith goals is like planning your garden for the future. Maybe you envision a garden filled with the flowers of deep Bible knowledge or strong personal character. Whatever your vision, remember that your goals will grow and change as you do, adapting to the different seasons of your life.

Let's talk about setting faith goals. Think about the aspects of faith you want to deepen. Do you want to understand the Bible better? Share your faith with others more confidently. Or improve your prayer life. Once you have a clear idea, set specific, achievable goals. For example, if you want to enhance your Bible knowledge, your goal could be to read the entire Bible over a year or study a particular book in depth. Write these goals down in a special notebook or digital app dedicated to tracking your faith journey. Review and adjust your goals annually to reflect your growth and the new directions where God is leading you.

"Continue to grow in faith and love."

The journey of faith is lifelong, and the habits you form now lay the foundation for your spiritual future. Regular Bible study is one foundational habit that keeps you rooted in God's Word, helping you navigate life with His wisdom. Similarly, active involvement in church nurtures your faith and allows you to contribute to the faith journeys of others, weaving your thread into the larger tapestry of your faith community. These practices provide opportunities to experience God's presence and form relationships that enrich your life in immeasurable ways.

Continual learning is another vital aspect of your faith journey. Life constantly changes, bringing new questions about God, faith, and the world. Keep an open heart and mind to learn more about God through books, sermons, and Bible studies to help navigate these changes. This approach allows your faith to be firm and flexible, deeply rooted but able to bend without breaking in the storms of life. Share what you know with others, answer their questions, and offer them the same hope and guidance God provides.

Think about the legacy of faith you want to leave. How do you want to be remembered by friends, family, and your community? More importantly, what impact do you want your faith to have on the world around you? Living a life that reflects God's love and truth is the most powerful legacy you can leave.

Make choices every day that align with God's commands to love Him and love others. It might mean choosing kindness over anger, forgiveness over holding a grudge, or courage over fear. Each choice weaves another golden thread into the legacy you create, inspiring others.

As you look forward to the following chapters of your life, remember that each day is an opportunity to grow in faith and love. Your faith journey is a beautiful garden you tend with God. Each goal you set, each lesson you learn, and each choice you make for love and faith sows seeds that will bloom in ways you might not be able to imagine now. So, keep stepping forward, keep learning, and keep loving. God is with you every step of the way, ready to turn even the smallest seeds of faith into splendid gardens of life and hope.

As this chapter closes, reflect on your spiritual growth and look to the future, remembering that these steps lead toward a deeper, fuller life with God. Each goal, lesson, and act of love is a thread in God's beautiful tapestry woven through your life. As you turn the page, carry forward the commitment to grow, the curiosity to learn, and the courage to live your faith boldly and lovingly. The next chapter awaits, filled with new opportunities to live out the beautiful truths you've cultivated here.

ACTIVITY - CHAPTER 8

Scan the QR code to start the activity.

Conclusion

As we wrap up our journey together through *Grace and Growth: Devotional Readings for Tween Girls,* I want to reflect on our incredible adventure.

From our first steps in discovering how uniquely God has created each of us to navigate the often exciting and sometimes challenging waters of tween life with faith, this book has been a vessel for exploration and growth. We've journeyed from understanding our worth in Christ's eyes to tackling real-world issues like friendships, family dynamics, and personal challenges—all through the lens of faith.

Throughout these pages, we've covered essential topics that touch the heart of being a tween girl in today's world:

- **Identity and self-worth:** Learning to see ourselves as God sees us—wonderfully made and deeply loved.
- **Confidence and comparison:** Embracing our God-given traits and talents and resisting the urge to compare ourselves to others.
- **Navigating relationships:** Choosing friends wisely and cultivating relationships that encourage spiritual growth.
- **Dealing with challenges:** Finding strength and comfort in Scripture during tough times.

- **Growing in faith:** Deepening your relationship with God through prayer, worship, and service.

The key takeaway from our time together is this: This book serves as your companion and guide as you grow in faith and navigate the ups and downs of tween life. It's here to offer insights and encouragement, but most importantly, to remind you that your journey with God is deeply personal and always evolving.

As we turn the final page, remember that your journey doesn't end here. I encourage you to keep exploring, asking questions, and deepening your relationship with God. Dive into your Bible, engage with your community, and find a church or youth group where you feel at home. Seek mentors who can guide you and friends who will walk beside you in faith.

If you haven't started a journal, now is the perfect time to begin. Document your thoughts, list your prayers, and celebrate when you see God's answers. This practice will help you see how active and present God is in your life.

Here's a blessing for your future: May you always know you are never alone. May God's love light your path, and His wisdom guide your steps. Wherever your journey takes you, may you find joy knowing God is with you at every turn.

Lastly, from my heart to yours, I hope this book serves as more than words on pages. I pray it acts as a stepping stone toward a fulfilling, faith-filled life, rich with love and guided by the ever-present hand of God.

Walk boldly, live joyfully, and love deeply. God has incredible plans for you, and I am cheering you on every step of the way.

With love and blessings,

Monika
Graceful Growth

A Prayer for Every Girl

Dear Heavenly Father,

I lift every girl who reads this book and every girl around the world to You. You know each one by name and their hearts, dreams, and struggles. I pray that You surround them with Your love and give them a deep sense of Your presence.

Lord, guide them as they grow, helping them to understand how wonderfully and uniquely You have made them. When they face challenges or feel overwhelmed, remind them that You are always with them, ready to strengthen and comfort them. May they find courage in Your word, peace in Your promises, and joy in walking closely with You.

Help them to see themselves through Your eyes—beautiful, valuable, and deeply loved. Please encourage them to use their gifts and talents to bring light and hope to those around them. Let them reflect Your grace and love in everything they do.

Protect their hearts and minds from anything leading them away from You. Grant them wisdom to make choices that honor You and help them build friendships that encourage and support their faith journey.

Lord, as they navigate the ups and downs of life, may they grow stronger in their faith, more profound in their love for You, and more confident in the purpose You have for them. May they always remember that they are never alone, for You are with them every step of the way.

Bless them with a life full of love, purpose, and joy. May Your light shine brightly in them, guiding them through every season of their lives.

In Jesus' name,
Amen.

Hey there, amazing reader!
Review Us!
Loved the book? Take a quick moment to leave a review by scanning the QR code below. Your words can inspire other young girls just like you. Thanks for being part of this journey!

References

Six Bible Passages About Identity & Self-Worth
https://godsword.org/blogs/seed-planters/six-bible-passages-about-identity-self-worth

Helping Kids Overcome Envy
https://www.becomingminimalist.com/helping-kids-overcome-envy

20 Women of the Bible Who Impacted Their World
https://www.learnreligions.com/influential-women-of-the-bible-4023025

Scriptural Affirmations and Blessings to Speak Over Your ...
https://inspiredbyfamilymag.com/2019/10/31/scriptural-affirmations-for-kids

21 Important Bible Verses About Choosing Friends
https://biblereasons.com/choosing-friends

How can I resist peer pressure? - Active Christianity
https://activechristianity.org/6-ways-to-resist-peer-pressure

Forgiveness and Reconciliation in the Bible - Sunshyne Gray
https://sunshynegray.com/forgiveness-reconciliation

How to Set Biblical Boundaries as a Christian
https://equippinggodlywomen.com/community/christian-boundaries

What Does the Bible Say About Family Relationships?
https://www.openbible.info/topics/family_relationships

Tips for Communicating With Your Teen
https://childmind.org/article/tips-communicating-with-teen/

Blended Family and Step-Parenting Tips
https://www.helpguide.org/articles/parenting-family/step-parenting-blended-families.htm

A Story of Forgiveness: Joseph and His Brothers
https://www.christiandivinity.com/blogs/light-of-christ-blog/a-story-of-forgiveness-joseph-and-his-brothers

8 Time Management Tips for Students - Harvard Summer School
https://summer.harvard.edu/blog/8-time-management-tips-for-students

30 Encouraging Bible Verses to Overcome Worry and Anxiety
https://www.biblestudytools.com/topical-verses/worry-and-anxiety-bible-verses

How to handle a bully as a Christian
https://godsygirl.com/handle-a-bully-as-a-christian

Integrating Faith into Family Life: Practical Tips and Activities
https://triciagoyer.com/integrating-faith-into-family-life-practical-tips-and-activities

Some of the Best Devotionals to Build the Faith of Tween ...
https://club31women.com/best-devotionals-tween-teen-girls

11 Creative Ideas for Teaching Kids How to Pray
https://ministryspark.com/creative-ideas-teaching-kids-prayer

9 Interactive Bible Study Ideas for Youth Groups
https://get.tithe.ly/blog/9-interactive-bible-study-ideas-for-youth-groups

Spiritual Practices for Kids: Worship
https://gominno.com/blog/spiritual-practices-for-kids-worship

Social Media and Youth Mental Health
https://www.hhs.gov/surgeongeneral/priorities/youth-mental-health/social-media/index.html

Digital Citizenship and Having a Godly Witness Online
https://christianlife-waunakee.org/digital-citizenship-and-having-a-godly-witness-online

Teaching Kids to Be Smart About Social Media (for Parents)
https://kidshealth.org/en/parents/social-media-smarts.html

Youth faith formation in a digital age
https://pres-outlook.org/2020/06/youth-faith-formation-in-a-digital-age

Changes: 7 Biblical Lessons to Make Sense of Puberty
https://www.intoxicatedonlife.com/store/product/changes

What Does the Bible Say About Body Image?
https://www.openbible.info/topics/body_image

Helping your kids find new friendships after the big move
https://www.focusonthefamily.ca/content/helping-your-kids-find-new-friendships-after-the-big-move

Setting God-Centered Goals for the New Year
https://avirtuouswoman.org/setting-god-centered-goals

7 Examples of Kindness in the Bible that Will Inspire You.
https://madeofstill.com/2022/03/13/kindness-in-the-bible

Teaching Kids About Stewardship: All My Stuff Belongs To ...
https://cogop.org/children/teaching-kids-about-stewardship-all-my-stuff-belongs-to-god

What does the Bible say about thankfulness/gratitude?
https://www.gotquestions.org/Bible-thankfulness-gratitude.html

The Courage to Lead by Example
https://herviewfromhome.com/the-courage-to-lead-by-example

Kistner, H. (2015). Praying the Psalms. St. Anthony Messenger, 123(1), 24-27.

Milton Keynes UK
Ingram Content Group UK Ltd.
UKHW022139051124
450708UK00016B/1418

9 798227 090652